The
Chipped
Cup

Many Blessings,
Kate Lynn Winters

Kate Lynn Winters

ISBN 978-1-63630-160-0 (Paperback)
ISBN 978-1-63630-161-7 (Digital)

Covenant Books
11661 Hwy 707
Murrells Inlet, SC 29576
www.covenantbooks.com

To my beloved sister and her children who hold a cherished place in my heart especially as we traveled on this journey together.

PROLOGUE

To those of you turning the pages, I invite you into a time in my life when I thought I would never see light again. My husband was afraid he may have lost me forever. Through my perseverance and commitment to my family and Lord, I was pulled out of my darkness. My intention of sharing my journey with you is to offer hope and encouragement. In times of despair, trust in God to transform your darkness into his marvelous light.

CHAPTER 1

It started out as an ordinary Thursday morning until it wasn't. I parked my car at work and looked down at my phone. I noticed a missed call from my niece. I thought that was odd since it was so early in the morning for her to call me. I listened to her brief message immediately knowing from the tone of her voice that something was terribly wrong.

As I nervously dialed her number, I was trying to convince myself that I was overreacting. She answered her phone quickly and I asked her, "Is everything okay?" She simply replied, "No." The next few words I heard stopped me in my tracks, and I stood still frozen like a statue. She told me that she was at the hospital all night with her mother, my sister Angela, and Angela was in the operating room undergoing emergency surgery. My sister suffered a major stroke and the doctor needed to perform surgery to remove a large clot from her brain. I could not believe what I was hearing. I asked Nicole, "Is she okay?" and again she replied, "No."

I stood there in complete shock. I told my niece I would be on the next flight to New York. I moved to Virginia about two years prior to this phone call. I wish I could have just blinked my eyes to be with my niece and sister at that very moment. Nicole told me that before my sister went into surgery, my sister told her to tell me not to fly up to New York right away, but to wait for things to get under control. *Under control, what does that mean?* I wanted to get more details from my niece, but she was so upset and exhausted, so we ended the phone call. All I wanted to do was to be there for both of them. I then called my husband, brother, and mother. They told me to just wait until she was out of surgery.

I replayed the last conversation I had with my sister a few days earlier. I knew that she wasn't feeling well and had been experiencing strange symptoms. She told me that she had a chilling sensation that ran up her spine. She also mentioned how exhausted she was feeling. She had gone to the doctor several times in the past weeks. Angela was not the type to call out sick from work unless it was totally necessary. She was a dedicated worker and held a high position at her bank.

I remember telling her that she needed to feel better because we were planning our upcoming family vacation soon. Every summer we go on vacation with extended family and friends. The reunion was a highlight for all of us. My family has always been very close and truly enjoy one another's company. We can be very silly at times to say the least, but we are also hard workers with strong family values instilled in us by our parents.

Angela promised me that she would feel better for our vacation as she was looking forward to our trip. Then she mentioned that her leg was swollen. I work in the medical field and I was very concerned with her symptoms. I told her to go back to the doctor right away and that she needed an ultrasound for her leg. We ended the conversation saying, "I love you." She scheduled another appointment with her doctor, but unfortunately she would not be able to keep that upcoming appointment.

My sister returned home from work that evening and still was not feeling well. A little later, my niece Nicole came home feeling apprehensive. She was worried that my sister would be mad at her as Nicole forgot to take the laundry out of the dryer before she left the house. Nicole was pleasantly surprised to see her mom cooking and that she was in a good mood. Angela made herself an egg sandwich and was sitting down getting ready to eat. Before she was able to take a bite of her sandwich, she started to yell out for Nicole to come help her. Angela was crying in agonizing pain that was shooting down her arm. She was not able to stand as her whole body became numb and paralyzed. Her speech slurred and panic gripped my niece. Nicole cried out, "Mom, you are scaring me!" Nicole dialed 911 although my sister was protesting for her not to call. My young nephew Tommy sat still on the couch and nervously witnessed the whole event.

The ambulance quickly arrived. The medics knew immediately that she was having a stroke. As Angela was being placed in the ambulance, her husband came home with my other niece, Amanda. Nicole hopped in the ambulance. Her father said he would follow in his car. Angela was amazingly calm in the ambulance and even winked at Nicole. She gave Nicole a thumbs-up when the medic said that she did a good job by calling 911.

The ambulance arrived at the closest hospital where a CAT scan was promptly performed. The doctor came out quickly and informed my niece of the devastating results. Angela had a large blood clot in her brain that needed to be removed immediately. She had to be transferred to a different hospital suited to perform such surgery. They transferred her into another ambulance, and she was brought to the awaiting hospital.

While my sister was getting the CAT scan, her husband Tom told my niece that he had to go out. He said he needed to get something to eat, leaving Nicole alone. He did not return for over an hour. Nicole was frantically waiting for his return. Nicole was not allowed to go into the second ambulance with her mother. She had no choice but to wait for her father because he had the car. She also wanted to let him know which hospital my sister was taken to. Nicole felt distraught not being with her mother knowing how scared she must have been. When Tom finally arrived back at the emergency room, Nicole told him they had to go to the next hospital right away. Nicole was upset and anxious, while Tom was calm and acting nonchalant.

Upon arriving at the second hospital, Nicole found the room her mother was in, but she was not allowed to enter. From the hallway, she could hear my sister screaming out in excruciating pain. Finally when Nicole was allowed into the room, she ran up to my sister's bedside trying to comfort her. Nicole was apologizing to her for leaving and explained that she was not allowed to ride in the ambulance. Minutes later, Angela was whisked off for emergency surgery. The surgery lasted over five hours. Nicole sat in the waiting room in shock for hours. Her father sat there watching television. Nicole pleaded with him to go find out if there were any updates. Hours before this surgery, Angela was a vibrant woman so full of life, and now she was barely holding on to her life.

The night dragged into early morning. The doctor finally came out to tell Tom and Nicole that the surgery went well and Angela pulled through. They were able to successfully remove the clot. The doctor said that my sister was going to recover and would just need physical therapy. However, she had a major stroke and was completely paralyzed on her left side of her body. She was not able to move her arm or leg. She could not speak partly because there was a breathing tube placed in her, but her speech was sufficiently affected by the stroke. Her neck and limbs were extremely swollen so much that they had to cut off her wedding rings on her finger. As soon as Nicole heard all the updates from the doctor, she called me.

My sister is my best friend and is like a second mother to me. She is the oldest child of our family taking me under her wing as we were growing up. I adored her and would follow her around like a puppy. As we grew older, we grew even closer. Anyone who met us could easily see the special bond we shared. She knew I would fly up in a heartbeat to be there, but she was practical. She wanted me to stay put and be there for my family as well. I was so torn. *Should I fly up because that is what my heart is telling me or do I respect my sister's wishes and wait?* I decided to wait and see what the next few hours would bring.

I felt like a zombie and was numb. I don't know how I worked that day. Honestly, I do not know how I worked for the next year, but I did. Just like my sister, I am a hardworking responsible person. In my office, there were many employees who would call out for every little thing, but that was not my style. I just concentrated on my work without speaking to any coworkers. I knew if I said a word, I would fall apart. As soon as I had a lunch break, I ran outside to be alone with my tears.

I immediately called my niece and brother for any new updates. My twin brother, Jeffrey, also worked in the medical field, and fortunately he worked close by. He was at the hospital every day supporting my niece and sister. Angela woke up from surgery panicking when she realized that she had a breathing tube in her throat and was hooked up to the ventilator breathing machine. Naturally she was very scared and obviously could not speak. The nurses gave her a notebook to see if she could write, but she was only able to scribble. The writing was very abstract and unclear. How damaged was her brain from the stroke? Jeffrey brought her much comfort and calmness reassuring her of what the doctors said. He told her that she had a stroke but would be all right after she had physical therapy. He told her that her surgery was successful and it was normal procedure for her to be on all these machines. She managed to write the letter "Y" in the notebook trying to ask my brother, "Why did this happen?" Of course, that was a question we all wanted the answer to.

CHAPTER 2

Even before we moved, I knew in my heart that there would come a time that my decision to leave New York would create stress for me. I always want to be there to support my family, especially in times of trouble. A few years prior, my husband came into our living room and he told me, "Oh, honey, you know what? Steve and Rick [friends of ours] are moving to Virginia. They are selling their house in Florida and plan to move."

I casually looked up from the book I was reading and said, "Really? That's great because I was planning on moving there too in a few years."

He replied, "Oh, I didn't know that."

I said, "Yes, Angela and I were talking about moving the past few months, and we are planning to check out different areas in Virginia."

Easygoing husband of mine replied, "Okay."

Both my sister and I kept hearing over and over from different customers and patients throughout the years that they were moving to Virginia. We were wondering what drew all these people to move from New York to Virginia. At this point, I was considering moving once my twin boys were finished with grammar school. They loved their school, and I wanted to wait until they had to transition into a new school. Their elementary school was excellent, but the middle schools and high schools in our neighborhood were not the greatest. I had a great job in a private medical office with a radiologist with whom I knew for over fifteen years. She was like a sister to me as well. I was respected at my job and it felt like family there. I worked very hard, but my work hours allowed me to be home before my children arrived home from school. My husband worked at the airport as a bartender and was doing very well.

I dated my husband when I was in college. We broke up for ten years but we stayed friends. We continued to see each other socially and even go on vacations together. We started dating again after the ten-year split. Our wedding was at our family vacation resort that we visit every summer. It was so much fun because our guests slept over and we continued the party the next morning. We were doubly blessed with beautiful identical twin boys, Ethan and Ryan. In New York, we lived in an apartment in a quiet courtyard with wonderful neighbors. Our neighbors who lived above us became a second set of grandparents to our children as they grew up. We lived within a few miles of my sister Angela, so my children were very close with their cousins.

My niece Nicole was the firstborn grandchild in our family. I have always felt a strong bond with her since she was born. I spent hours babysitting and I loved spending time with her. Since her birth, I always knew she was an extremely special person. My sister had another precious daughter Amanda who was four years younger than Nicole and then a six-year span before she had her son Tommy. Her son was a year younger than my twins. The three of them loved being together. They became very close as well and were more like brothers than cousins. When little Tommy was with us spending time with the twins, I felt like I had triplets rather than twins. The rest of my family and my husband's family lived nearby as well. Both of our families enjoy spending time together. Sadly, my husband's parents were both very sick and passed away early in his life. My parents became like a second set of parents to my husband.

My parents were very welcoming. As a child, our house was the house everyone hung out at. My mother was sweet and kind. My father was full of life and humor. As children, we were afraid of my father because he appeared intimidating, but he was a big teddy bear on the inside. I had childhood friends from first grade who also lived close by in our neighborhood. My husband and I had many mutual friends nearby as well.

So why move? We were not moving away from anything negative. We had good jobs, a nice apartment, lovely neighbors, long-standing friends, and devoted families. We never moved out of the state before, and it was going to be a big change. We were moving to a place where we knew no one and did not have jobs there yet. I knew that my sister was planning on moving as well. As much as I liked where we lived, I wanted to be able to buy a house for my children. I could never afford New York prices and the housing market was only increasing. I wanted my children to attend a better and safer middle school. I figured if we sold our apartment in New York, we could afford a really nice new house in Virginia. I felt a pull to move. I knew it was going to be one of the hardest decisions of my life. I loved my life in New York and so did my children.

Ethan and Ryan are identical and very much alike in many ways. They are resistant to any changes. When they were four, we remodeled our apartment, and they were both upset for the longest time because they missed their old bathtub. I knew that this move was going to be rough on them.

CHAPTER 3

The following week after my sister's surgery, my niece continued to go to work as well. She managed to visit my sister daily before or after her shift. I still wanted to be there, but my mother advised me to wait out the week before flying up. The following weekend was the Fourth of July, which would allow me extra time for my visit.

The week of waiting was pure torture. Every minute and hour of the day dragged on. I could not eat or sleep, but I managed to make it through each work day. As soon as I got home, I would curl up in the fetal position on the couch and cry uncontrollably. I still did not mention any of this to my coworkers; I could not handle the office gossip. I just kept quiet and to myself all week. I managed to call one of my friends. She told me to go to New York sooner and that I would never forgive myself if something happened. That made me feel even worse. There were days with little or no new information on test results or updates. Unlike a medical television show, where the diagnosis is wrapped up in one hour, that was not our reality.

Angela had been in the hospital for over a week now and was still not breathing on her own. Her condition seemed worse because they had to place a new tube into her neck instead of her mouth. The doctors had to surgically cut a hole into her throat to place the tube that was attached to the ventilator. The ventilator became her life support. Her handwriting improved some as she used multiple notebooks to write, which was the only way she was able to communicate. She started to write to Nicole telling her what errands she wanted her to run. We took that as a good sign because a bit of her old personality was showing through. She asked Nicole to call her job and update them. She was also worried about her children. At this point, the doctors were still saying that once the trach tube was removed, all she would need was physical therapy and could go home again. It didn't make sense to me. How could that be possible when she is on life support?

Toward the end of the week, Nicole finally found out there was a mass in her mother's chest. She told me the doctor did not know what type of tumor it was. I almost collapsed at the news. I couldn't understand why it took so long to find out about this mass; it had to be seen on the initial CAT scan the night of the stroke. I called my brother to question him about this chest mass. He said he would try to get more information from the doctors, but they were working on stabilizing her. She was still in critical condition and kept going in and out of consciousness. My brother's presence at the hospital daily brought comfort to my sister and niece. He became their supportive rock and explained all the medical lingo to them. I was proud of him and I also took comfort in his being there for them.

After hearing about the lung mass, I immediately went on the computer to start my search. My first thought was cancer, but I searched for other possibilities. My sister was recently remodeling her bathroom. She told me that there was black mold when they ripped out the bathtub. I searched for fungal infection and read that a fungal infection could appear as a solid mass in the lung. I mentioned this to Nicole trying to convince both of us that maybe Angela would be cured once she gets the proper treatment.

As much as I did not want to work every day, it provided a distraction for me. During my lunch break, I would run outside to be alone to cry. I could barely run out the door fast enough to release the tears that were welling in my eyes. If I had a small break in the day, I would sit with the lights turned down and pray. Praying always brought me comfort. When my father was diagnosed with cancer, he prayed the rosary daily. I believe his faith supported him through the years as he dealt with the many struggles he had to endure. I held his rosary ring tightly as I prayed for my sister's recovery.

I am a firm believer in the power of prayer. My parents were devout Catholics and religion became an important part of our lives. When I was younger, we had to sit with our classmates at Sunday Mass. Each child had their own little envelope for the collection basket. My parents would give us a quarter to put into our little envelopes. Religious events were even more special because my uncle was involved in them. He was a priest and a special uncle who adored us. He performed our Baptisms, First Holy Communion and our weddings. My wedding was the last one that he was able to celebrate.

When we were children, we would have pretend church services in our basement, inviting all our neighborhood friends. We dressed up our dolls and held make-believe Baptisms. One time, I dressed up my poor cat in a white gown and he was baptized as well. One of my most cherished childhood photographs is one where my sisters are dressed like nuns, my twin brother dressed as a priest and for some reason, I was dressed as Santa Claus. Angela and I always cracked up at that combination. It didn't take much for us to laugh and find humor in just about anything. That humor was part of our special bond. My family definitely has a unique sense of humor. We manage to have a good time no matter where we are as long as we are together.

CHAPTER 4

I was still living in New York during the horrifying incomprehensible events of 911. My heart still breaks for all those families that had to endure the unthinkable horrors and trauma of that day. I remember the panic I felt that morning. I lived only several miles from Manhattan where both my brother and sister were working that morning. We could see and smell the black smoke from the tower's collapse for weeks in our neighborhood. Thoughts of that day still send chills up my spine. It took a toll on me emotionally, and I became fearful of flying alone. I was determined to get on the plane to be with my sister no matter what.

My husband dropped me off at the airport at five o'clock Saturday morning July 3rd. My flight was scheduled for six thirty. I sat anxiously waiting, keeping my eyes glued to the flight board. I freaked out when I saw my flight was cancelled. I jumped up and ran to the counter where a long line had already formed. I found out that all the flights were cancelled and there were no flights until the next day. My mind went crazy. I knew I could not wait another day after this brutal week to see my sister.

I inquired about flights to different airports but was told there were no flights available at all. I pleaded with the customer representative who then directed me to a different service desk. I ran across the hallway to the service desk and was faced with another long line. At this point, I could not fight back my tears. I desperately explained that my sister was critically ill and I needed a flight today. Of course, the conversation with my friend popped into my mind. I started thinking maybe she was right and I should have left sooner. The representative at this service counter was not very helpful either. I asked, "Can I get a flight anywhere that can bring me closer to New York? Are there any flights to New Jersey or Connecticut?" She could tell that I was not budging. Finally she managed to get me a flight to New Jersey. I was just relieved that at least I could get onto a flight even though it meant waiting a few more hours. I would figure out a way to get to New York once I landed.

I sat there for hours anxiously staring at the clock until it was time to board. I handed in my boarding pass. The flight agent looked at me and said, "I'm sorry but you cannot come on this flight. The seat that they gave you is already taken." I started to cry hysterically pleading with her, "Please I beg you. I need to get on this flight." With each sentence, the pitch of my voice rose as I explained that my other flight was cancelled and I was given this new flight. I had been waiting for hours and I had to get to New York today. I told her that my sister may be dying and I will sit anywhere on the plane. At this point, everyone in line was staring at me. I was about to lose it, but by the grace of God, she took pity on me. She left the counter and came back with the news that she managed to get me a seat on the plane. I was so grateful! After the plane landed, I took a taxi to get to New York. I finally arrived at the hospital rushing through the doors around 1:00 p.m.

I took a deep breath and entered my sister's room. She was in a private cramped room lying in the bed facing the window. She was hooked up to the breathing machine with various intravenous tubes attached to her. With barely enough space, I squeezed around the machine to try to embrace her. The breathing tube was surgically placed in the middle of her throat with tape holding it in place. I could clearly see how critical her health was. She was able to mouth some words but still had no control of the left side of her body. Her neck was so swollen that it resembled a tree stump.

She opened her eyes and recognized me. I gave her a huge hug wiping away tears from my face. My other sister and mother arrived within the hour. It was so nice to see them and I hugged them as well. My sister Debra was telling me how Angela kept speaking of this young girl in the room. Angela said the girl appeared often and she resembled her youngest daughter, Amanda. In reality, no young girl ever visited her at the hospital.

As I went to sit down at the foot of the bed, I could see my sister was clearly getting upset. She was flaring her right hand for me to get up. I jumped off the bed immediately thinking I was making her more uncomfortable. I apologized because I didn't want to add any additional discomfort to her. She shook her head and mouthed to me, "No, that's not it. You were sitting where the pretty young child was sitting." I then pulled up a chair instead and sat near the head of the bed.

My sister slept most of the day as much as she could with the constant stream of nurses coming in and out of the room. They had to keep suctioning her throat to retrieve the mucous and blood that was constantly accumulating. I asked if I could speak with a doctor regarding her condition because I had so many questions. I was told that there wasn't any doctor available at the moment. It was very difficult to get information from any of the hospital staff.

I didn't think my sister was actually sleeping but was just going in and out of consciousness. I started to look through her notebooks from the past week, but most of the writing was unrecognizable. I was able to pick out a few words here and there. It looked like a three-year-old trying to write. My sister was physically here on earth because I was looking right at her, but I was beginning to think that her soul was in between both realms. Her body was here trapped in a hospital bed, but was her soul elsewhere at certain moments?

My sister had a late-term miscarriage before she was pregnant with my oldest niece, Nicole. I had to wonder maybe this young girl she kept seeing was her first child. Was this daughter sent from above to keep her company? As I stood there staring at my sister, a strange calmness came over me. The room was quiet except for the respirator hissing away. My sister opened her eyes. She turned to me and said, "The nurses keep telling me that I am hallucinating when I speak of the young girl in the room." The nurses knew how critical my sister was, and they probably thought she had brain damage from the stroke. I didn't feel that way and I told my sister that I believed her. I believed the young beautiful girl was an angel God sent to watch over her. My sister slowly nodded in agreement. Then Angela pointed and told me that the girl was standing right beside me in the room and shivers ran down my body.

Naturally I looked side to side and saw no one there. I asked my sister, "Is she standing right next to me now?"

My sister nodded yes. Angela said, "Oh, she is so nice but she can't hand me my ChapStick like you can."

I softly laughed and replied, "Yes, you are right." Anyone who has ever met my sister would immediately pick up on one of her quirky habits of uncapping her Chapstick, gliding it on her lips making a soft smacking sound and then dramatically recapping it.

I left the hospital very late and took the train to my mother's house. I returned to the hospital early the next day. Later in the morning my niece Nicole arrived at the hospital with her father. I was overjoyed to see Nicole and my heart went out to her. Nicole and I share a closeness similar to the relationship I had with my sister. She knew she could always rely on me. Nicole had confided in me over the years about family issues, mostly involving her father, Tom. For all of the twenty-five years I knew Tom, I experienced him as the "life of the party". This seemed fine with my sister while they were dating. Once they got married and started a family, the partying didn't work out too well.

When I was younger, I had a suspicious mind about people and would sense the bad in them. Angela would only see the good in people. She had a tendency to trust more openly. My sister is the polar opposite of her husband. She may have a few drinks but that was the limit. When they were newlyweds, Angela would work full time and continued her studies for her master's degree. She would stay home at night to study, while Tom would go out to party.

Before they were married, I remember Angela waking me up around 3:00 a.m. I asked her, "What's wrong?" She was in a panic and told me that she could not find Tom. He said he was going to meet her but did not show up. She whispered to me that she was nervous because he was doing a lot of cocaine lately. She was so concerned that maybe he was hurt somewhere. I told her that I was sure he was fine but that did not satisfy her. She asked me if I would go with her to look in the different bars that he hung out at to try to find him. I was still in high school and underage, so I did not think I would be able to get into the bars, but she wanted me to keep her company. Of course, I couldn't say no to her. I got out of bed and we started perusing the neighborhood in search of Tom but did not have any success after hours of searching. We wanted to get home before our parents woke up.

CHAPTER 5

The day I arrived in New York, Nicole wanted to stay at the hospital with me all day. I told her that I was finally here and that she should take a break. Tom's sister Donna was hosting her annual Fourth of July party. I insisted that Nicole go and try to relax. It took a lot of convincing but she finally agreed. I am sure she did not relax but at least maybe she could be distracted for a few hours. The constant not knowing and waiting for answers takes a toll on your mind. Since it was a holiday weekend, there was limited staff and I still could not find any nurse or doctor willing to talk to me. It was so frustrating.

Angela asked for her reading glasses and the book she had been reading before the stroke. I helped her put on her glasses as she attempted to read her book. I will always remember that moment of her expressing her strength. She wanted to maintain a normal appearance so that I would believe she was going to be all right. She was always there for me whenever I had a problem. She was my rock and she continued to never let me down.

The following night while she was resting, I stepped out of the room to speak to my brother-in-law Tom. I told him about my bathroom fungal theory. I was explaining to him that if the mass was from a fungal infection, Angela needed treatment and would be cured. He shook his head saying, "No, that's not it."

I replied, "How do you know that's not it? They have not done a biopsy yet."

He kept being vague, so I continued to press him. I kept questioning my brother-in-law until he finally confessed that the doctor said it was cancer. He knew this information the first night of the stroke after the CAT scan was performed at the emergency room. He chose not to share any of this information with us. The doctor told him the tumor was cancerous and that was the reason for the clots, which led to the stroke.

I felt weak in my knees. I turned abruptly away from him and ran back into her room. My mind was racing; I had built up my hopes all week with my fungal theory only to find out it was all in vain. I felt like a fool and felt horrible giving Nicole false hope. Meanwhile her father knew the truth and withheld this crucial information for the entire week.

The following day, I continued sitting at my sister's bedside. I had to catch my flight back later that evening. The nurse came in and told me she was going to disconnect the breathing tube for a few minutes to see if Angela could speak. The nurse wanted to ask her a few questions to see how she responded. Then she left the room. At this point, no one knew at what level my sister's brain was functioning at. My brother was outside in the car waiting for me to drive me to the airport. I could not bear to tear myself away because I desperately needed to hear her voice. I hated to keep my brother waiting and I knew I had a flight to catch, but I could not leave just yet.

Everything that happened in the hospital felt like slow motion. Each minute I waited for the nurse to return felt like an hour. She finally entered the room to disconnect the breathing tube.

She asked my sister, "Do you know who the President of the United States is?"

Angela replied, "Yes. Obama."

I was in tears when I heard her speak. I quickly kissed her goodbye and ran out of the room. I met my brother and shared the good news.

CHAPTER 6

I returned home and went to work the next day exhausted. During that week, my coworkers knew something was definitely wrong with me. I am usually very upbeat and personable, but I continued to keep to myself. I noticed a small piece of white paper outside of my office, so I bent down and picked it up. I flipped it over and read the typed words on the paper, "Hold those that you love dear. Precious is the time we share. Do not wait for tomorrow, for tomorrow may not be." Chills went down my spine as I stood still in the hallway. I felt this was a message from my deceased father trying to communicate with me. Then I reread the message with a sinking feeling that he was trying to tell me that my sister was going to die.

I decided to confide in a friend at work, but I made her swear that she could not share this information. She promised she would not. I showed her the piece of paper and how I thought it was a sign from my father telling me my sister was going to die. My friend did her best to try to convince me that I was misinterpreting the message and that my sister was going to be fine. During lunch, I found another piece of paper outside on the ground. I was compelled to pick it up. I flipped the paper over and it had information for grief counseling services for children who had suffered a loss of a loved one. The knot in my stomach grew tighter.

Time stood still as I waited on any updates on my sister's progress. The information was scarce as the doctors were still trying to stabilize her enough to perform a lung biopsy. It would be another high risk procedure requiring anesthesia. The doctor expressed concern that she may not survive the biopsy. I was planning on driving to New York that Friday for our family vacation. I just needed to get through the next four days at work.

As I was heading to my car, I received a call from my brother. I could tell from the tone of his voice that he had bad news to deliver. I held my breath waiting to hear that my sister had passed away. Instead, he told me that the biopsy was complete and Angela made it through the procedure. He hesitated telling me that the doctor had the results of the biopsy. My sister had lung cancer. I stood there frozen in the exact location where I spoke to Nicole a few weeks prior. It felt like I was punched in the gut and I wanted to vomit. I started to cry again not knowing how I had any tears left in me.

I cried all the way home and then managed to pack for our trip. We drove the next morning for nine hours to New York. As soon as we arrived in New York, we headed over to the hospital. Angela was moved to a different room called the step-down unit which was for less critical patients. I thought that was a positive change since last time and maybe she was more stable. I prayed that she would be able to get treatment for her cancer and physical therapy.

This room was occupied by three other patients divided by curtains. Her bed was closest to the door. Angela seemed more mentally alert than the week before. She smiled when she saw me, my husband, and children. She was still hooked up to all of her machines but was able to communicate better with her writing. The room was crowded as we squeezed in to hug her. She wrote in her notebook that she loved my sons. She really did adore them and they loved their aunt. My husband is very close to my sister as well and has been a part of her life for over twenty-five years.

I could see a bit of her sense of humor shining through. She wrote in her notebook that there was a rhino in the room with her. I did not understand what that meant. Later that evening, I heard this strange honking, coughing noise. It was coming from the patient behind the curtain next to my sister's bed. My sister mouthed to me, "That's the rhino." I smiled and giggled.

There were some amazing nurses in that unit and my sister thanked them in her notebook. Unfortunately, there was a nurse's aide who was not very nice. Angela asked me if I could get her underwear. There was only a curtain separating her and the male patients in the room. Most of the time, the nurses left the curtains wide open. The nurse's aid was adamant about her not wearing underwear. Angela said she is a lady and wanted to wear them. I told her that I would find out about the underwear from the nurse. Then the aid abruptly pulled the curtain open exposing Angela's half-covered body to everyone in the room. There was a male patient with his visiting family members straight across from my sister's bed viewing the whole ordeal. I immediately covered her up. I held my tongue even though I was very angry at her.

Angela kept coughing because of the mucus and blood that would constantly accumulate in her throat. She coughed really hard and some urine leaked out. The aid said in a really nasty tone to her, "See, now you are incontinent!" Angela's eyes grew wide open in fear. I told my sister that she was not incontinent.

I declared to everyone in the room, "She just coughed very hard. That was all." I turned to the aid and asked her, "Can you not see what condition she is in? I would appreciate it if you kept your comments to yourself." It took all my control because I really wanted to jump across the bed and strangle this woman.

I spent the next few days at her bedside in this cramped stepdown unit room still waiting for new information. A nice young medical resident came in to examine her. He asked me if I wanted to see her CAT scan. I replied yes. I was so excited and thankful that someone was willing to share information with me. He had a portable computer, which he was able to pull up her CAT scan images. We huddled in the middle of the room.

When I saw the image, I knew how terminal her cancer was. There was a massive solid tumor located centrally in her chest. He then explained to me that surgery was not an option; it would have been different if the mass was in a lobe of either lung. They could remove a lung, but Angela's mass was smack in the middle of her chest, and therefore surgery was not an option. The mass was indeed very large but that was not the only problem. He pointed out the multiple lymph nodes traveling up her sternum. The combination of the tumor along with the gigantic lymph nodes was putting pressure on and compressing her blood vessels. That was the reason her neck and face were swollen. The only positive was that her abdominal CAT scan did not show any other evidence of cancer that could have traveled to her liver or other organs. Looking at actual images, I knew that it would take a miracle for her to ever leave the hospital.

The resident explained that they could try radiation therapy to shrink the mass. If the mass were smaller, they may be able to perform surgery; however, she was too unstable to undergo radiation at this point. There were more tests scheduled to determine if the lung cancer was Stage 3 or Stage 4, Stage 4 being the worst-case scenario. My sister was only two feet away from us. I didn't want her to see my reaction, so I kept my back to her. I sincerely thanked him. He was the first person who took the time to talk to me honestly.

We returned to her bedside. He said he was trying to find her a better room. He asked her if there was anything he could do for her. She asked him if it was possible to take her bed out of this room and go for a ride in the hallway. She was tired of being in this room all week and wanted a different view.

He replied, "Yes, we can do that later."

I asked her, "Do you really want to go for a ride in the hallway?" She nodded.

We brought her a round-neck pillow to try to ease her discomfort. She told me that she was going to wear the pillow as a crown and wave like a queen when she went for her ride through the halls. I gently placed the pillow on her head and she did a queen's wave pose. I snapped a picture of her with my phone. She was trying to be her normal silly self with me and we shared a giggle. Those images of her CAT scan flashed into my mind, and I knew nothing would be normal again.

The physical therapist was able to assist her to sit in an upright position after much struggle on my sister's part. Angela managed to sit on the side of the bed. It took over half an hour to achieve this with much encouragement. It was a bigger feat for her to stand. She managed to stand but for only a minute. Angela had been lying down in bed for weeks, and the exertion of moving made her extremely dizzy. She was exhausted from standing. She wrote in her notebook that it would have been better if she died instead of being like this. That broke my heart. I shook my head and told her that wasn't so. Then she wrote that she wanted me to raise her son with my husband and that she had a will. I knew she wanted me to raise her children if anything happened to her because we discussed this many years ago when our children were younger. I also knew that in her will, I was named the legal guardian, but that was in the event both parents died. I was not going to get into all this with her.

I leaned into her and whispered into her ear, "I promise I will do everything possible so that I can raise your son and take care of your daughters." I reassured her about her children and told her that she did not have to worry. I told her that all she needed to do was rest and concentrate on getting better.

That evening, both my brothers, sister, and mother came to the hospital and we really had to squeeze around the bed. My brother just came from a dinner date. Angela was inquiring about how it went. She wanted him to meet someone special. He had been married twice already. I told him that if he was considering marriage again, he needed the approval from me and Angela. She nodded her head in agreement. I was trying to lighten the atmosphere, so I joked with my brother. I said that we do not want him to have as many marriages compared to how many times he needed to take the road test to get his driver's license. It took him four tries before he passed his road test. I knew my brother would be a good sport about the joke. We heard my sister's hearty laugh even though it was muffled from the breathing tube. It felt so good to hear her laugh and was a true gift to us that night.

My sister managed to write a message for my mother in her notebook. She wrote, "Mom, you are a good mom. You raised your children to care for and love each other." That evening and those words touched my soul. Here was my sister laying in critical condition sharing such beautiful words to my mother. It was a profound moment. Even in our darkest moments in life, beautiful memories can arise. I felt my sister's words to my mother was the highest compliment a person could receive. I included my sister's loving words in my mother's eulogy when my sweet mother passed.

The following evening, Angela was assigned a new room and was waiting for transport. When her husband arrived, he asked her if she needed anything. She said she would like more pillows and he said he would find some. I told him to wait because transport was on their way to move her. He told me not to worry. He said he would find us and ran out of the room. A few minutes later, the transport came to move her. The move was quick as they expertly maneuvered her bed with the attached machines through the hallways and into a private room. It was very late in the evening. I just stared out the window into the dark Manhattan skyline. Hours slowly passed with no sign of my brother-in-law. My sister was very uncomfortable and not doing well after the move. Every task took a toll on her. My brother-in-law finally showed up in the doorway and I asked him, "Where are the pillows?"

He replied, "What pillows?"

CHAPTER 7

Over the next few days, her physical state was unchanged, but there were times when her spirit would be more present. It felt like the first time I saw her at the hospital when she was in and out of consciousness. I had a sinking feeling that she was not going to make it through the night. I could not bear to leave her, so I decided to stay. I curled up in the chair next to the bed trying to sleep. I held her hand all night long and would not let go. Something nudged me awake. I looked at the television and saw an image of a beautiful field of wild dandelions. My sister made a soft sound. I immediately turned my attention to her and asked her if she was all right. She nodded peacefully.

Then I asked her, "Is Dad here in the room with us?" She nodded yes again. She wrote in her notebook that he is here, but he is not alone. There were fifty-two angels with him. Tearfully I asked her if she wanted to go with them. She shook her head no. I could feel a different energy in the room. I had been praying for weeks for her recovery, and now I was praying for her to leave this earth peacefully. I continued to hold her hand crying softly until she fell asleep again.

Surprisingly she made it through the night. She continued to undergo more rounds of various tests as well as endless needle stabbings for blood drawing. Each blood draw was difficult because her circulation and veins were compromised. Her hands and legs were swollen. It felt like Groundhog Day because each day at the hospital seemed just like the day before. The respiratory team would come in several times a day to suction out all the bloody mucus in her throat. The hissing noise of the ventilator was relentless. My sister had no food or liquids for several weeks. She continued to complain because she was so thirsty. We were able to give her ice chips but had to be careful because some of the fluid could enter her lungs instead.

Radiation treatment was finally scheduled to shrink her tumor. She managed to undergo three radiation treatments. It was an ordeal just to transport her through the hallways and to the basement where the radiation department was located. She still was not able to move half of her body. It took several people to transfer her to the radiation table. I did my best to try to keep her spirits up. It was tearing my heart out to see the anguish look on her face when they moved her.

I remained at her bedside all day trying my best to make her comfortable. I would massage her feet, hands, shoulders and back. I lifted her leg and arm up and down to decrease the swelling. I was concerned about muscle atrophy and bedsores. If she needed any-thing, I would communicate it to the nurses. I was her voice now. If she managed to doze off, I would sneak out of the room and go to the small quiet chapel in the hospital. I broke down in tears after immediately entering the chapel. I found some comfort being alone in this sacred place. On the altar was a book where people wrote their intentions. I could feel the presence of all those who had been in this chapel praying for their loved ones. I would sit in silence, praying for my sister and for all those who would be entering the chapel in the future.

CHAPTER 8

Nicole and I spent a lot of time together at the hospital. She started opening up to me about things that were going on in their house. It tore at my heart listening to the details of what they had been living through because of the actions of their father. There was constant tension, stress, and fighting because my brother-in-law would go out all night to party or disappear for days without a trace. There were harsh fights between her parents and screaming matches. I knew of his drug problem but not nearly to the extent of what Nicole was telling me. I knew Tom had stolen money in the past, but Nicole told me that he has been stealing money from her since she was a child. She had to hide her allowance and work money in a vitamin jar. He even took her prescription medication to sell.

I figured Tom would steal money to buy drugs. Then Nicole revealed that he has a serious gambling addiction. That was shocking news to hear. Angela would complain about finances and bills, which always struck me odd because she had an excellent job. Tom did work throughout the years but his work history was sketchy at times. No wonder why she was always stressed about money. Nicole overheard Tom pleading with my sister telling her that if he doesn't pay "them" back, then "they" would kill him. Angela took out a second mortgage on the house to pay back Tom's gambling debt. Now it was all making sense to me. Nicole said her father had not been working for over a year and that his drug and gambling addictions had escalated.

My mind was racing with each incident Nicole shared. My blood was boiling and I could barely contain myself. With each detail I learned, my anger built. I was trying to understand why my sister stayed with him and put up with all of this. I knew she loved him but she did not deserve to be treated this way and certainly neither did her children. Her children were innocent and did not deserve to grow up in this dysfunctional household. She chose to keep their lives a secret. I felt hurt and betrayed by her because she did not confide in me. I know it was her pride, but maybe I could have helped her.

I recalled a conversation I had with her several years ago. She told me that she had taken Tom's name off her retirement and life insurance plan as her beneficiary on the policies. She changed it to Nicole as the sole beneficiary. She said it was a process but Tom was in agreement. She told me that if anything ever happened to her, then her children would be provided for. I asked her why and what happened, but she would not tell me. I did not want to push her, so I just listened. I mentioned this to Nicole and we realized that must have been the time when she took out a second mortgage on the house. I figured at this point in her life the house was almost paid for.

I asked Nicole, "Was this the time when Tom said someone was going to kill him if he didn't pay his gambling debt?"

She replied, "Yes, but there was more to it."

She told me that her father was also cheating on Angela. Nicole said she found women's clothes in her hamper when she returned home early from our family vacation. Nicole came back a few days before Angela and Tom did not go that year. Tom removed their wedding picture from the wall. Angela also discovered thousands of dollars that he charged on the credit card. The charges were obvious that he spent money on his indiscretions. Tom made no attempt to cover his tracks not caring if my sister found out. He just came and went doing whatever he wanted.

Nicole told me that many mornings she would awake to find a random drunk man sleeping it off in the basement. My nieces shared a bedroom in the basement just a few feet away from where Tom's bar buddies would crash for the night. I was flabbergasted. I asked her, "Did Angela know any of this?" Nicole's reply was no. Angela would leave super early for work, while Tom slept it off on the couch upstairs in the living room.

For the next few weeks, the floodgates opened as Nicole continued to share more with me. My gut reaction was to confront my brother-in-law, but Nicole pleaded with me not to. She said when Tom is confronted, he becomes intimidating and violent. Nicole had witnessed many fights between her parents. Angela would not stop yelling at him pushing him to his limits which created dangerous encounters. He would shove her against the wall, and she would start throwing random household objects at him.

Nicole was physically shaking as she spoke to me. She said that she could not handle any more stress. She asked me not to confront him. She did not want anything to happen to me. I knew Tom had a temper from the past. I remembered a hole he punched in their apartment wall when they were newlyweds. Nicole told me that he will fly off the handle quickly especially if he was high or hung over. Angela had kept a picture hidden in her night table dresser that Nicole came across. It was a photo of my sister with a black eye. Nicole confronted her mother and Angela said she was keeping the picture as proof.

It took all my energy to refrain from confronting Tom when I saw him. I had to act like I knew none of this to respect Nicole's request. Although deep inside of me I wanted to hurt him. I was so angry that he not only hurt my sister emotionally but physically as well. He put all of his family through years of pain and suffering. I wanted him to suffer like he had made them suffer. The same man that I loved as my brother-in-law for over twenty-five years now was a man I despised.

When Tom did show up at the hospital, his behavior was frantic. He could not sit still and would pace the floor and speak a mile a minute. His nose was constantly running. I mentioned his behavior to Nicole. She said that is his normal behavior but had gotten much worse with his increased drug use. It made me think back to a time years prior when my sister did not meet me for Mass one Sunday. We would go to church together and then spend time drinking coffee and chatting at her house. I was concerned, so I drove to her house after church services.

When I arrived at the house, she was fine but told me that Tom was missing for two days. He was home now and was in the basement. Naturally, I asked her if she called the police to file a missing person's report. She nonchalantly replied, "No. He does this from time to time." I was confused and questioned her as to why he does this. She just shrugged her shoulders. I asked if she would mind if I spoke to him. She said, "Go ahead," and I headed down the stairs. He looked awful and was slumped over the couch.

I asked him, "Why are you doing this?" I told him he has a family that loves him and asked him, "Why are you choosing this lifestyle and throwing your family away?" He too just shrugged his shoulders with no reply. I told him that he needed professional help to figure out why he is acting like this. He nodded his head but never sought any help.

I marched upstairs to confront my sister. I thought this situation was outrageous. I told her that if he doesn't want to get help, then she needs to consider filing for a divorce. My sister got upset with me. She questioned me, "What was I supposed to do?" I told her that she should have called the police. I told her that when it happens again to call the police, file for a divorce, and change the locks. I was annoyed with both of them. I knew he did not want help and my sister was enabling him. I also knew my sister. Now that I confronted her, she probably would clam up and not tell me if he went missing again.

Angela was a private person and wanted the outside world to view her life as normal. I now understood the stress and pressure she was living with her entire married life. It was no wonder why she was lying here in critical condition. I had to push down the disgust I felt for Tom and try to focus only on my sister. It was a challenge to see him, but his hospital visits were becoming less frequent. I slept over at the house to keep an eye on my nephew. I knew I was getting under Tom's skin because he was being watched. He told Nicole he couldn't wait until I went back to Virginia.

CHAPTER 9

Angela desperately wanted her hair washed. The nurses told her that it was impossible in her condition. I was not going to accept that answer and found a way to wash her hair. She asked for a mirror so she could fix her hair. She told me that her bigwig bosses from the bank were visiting today and her best friend Susan was soon to arrive from California. They have been childhood friends, and Susan's personality is filled with sunshine. This lifted Angela's spirits tremendously.

The bosses arrived bringing her yellow roses. Angela wrote their names down to make proper introductions. It was easy to see how uncomfortable they were seeing her connected to the life support machine. I did my best to speak for her. I told them how much she loved the flowers. I explained that she was doing so much better compared to the weeks prior. She is building her strength back and that she had every intention of returning to work. She was nodding her head to show agreement. I was a bit nervous because I was speaking for her. I didn't want to upset her if I said the wrong thing. Their visit was brief. I asked Susan if what I said was all right. She replied, "It was perfect." Susan and I spent the next few days at my sister's bedside caring for her as our relationship grew closer.

At this point, my sister did not actually have a room. She had been moved from the previous room. Her bed was in a hallway holding area where they placed patients for postoperative recovery care. There were no walls, only curtains surrounding her. I was massaging her temples until she finally fell asleep. She was actually sleeping for the first time in such a long time. I quietly and gently pulled back the curtain to hop on a stretcher outside her makeshift room. I saw a young resident approaching. As he was about to pull the curtain open, I leapt off the stretcher to jump in front of him. I stopped him and asked, "What do you need to do?" I explained that she was finally sleeping. He said he needed her signature on some form. I asked him if it was possible to leave the form and I promised she would sign them when she woke up. Surprisingly, he agreed. I was now her advocate and protective watchdog.

Angela now had a proper bed in the ICU. It was necessary to insert a feeding tube because it had been weeks since she was able to eat. Angela was panicking when they came to place the tube. The doctor had to thread the feeding tube up into her nose and down her throat. While the tube was being placed, I spoke to her in a calm voice giving her instructions on how to breathe until the tube was successfully placed and taped securely onto her skin.

Susan was staying for the week and convinced me to take a little break. She told me to join my family at our vacation resort even for a night. I knew she was right as I recalled the same conversation I had when I convinced Nicole that she needed to take a break. Susan reassured me that she would take great care of my sister. I drove upstate but was filled with anxiety, especially since the cell phone reception was lousy at the resort.

I was surprised when my phone actually rang. Unfortunately, it was an urgent phone call from the nurse because the feeding tube fell out. They needed to reinsert a new one and my sister was freaking out. Angela told the nurse that I needed to be there and she could not tolerate the procedure without me. Susan was at the bedside and she was in a panic as well. The doctor was in the room at that moment and wanted to reinsert the feeding tube. There was no way they would wait three hours for me to drive back. I asked the nurse if I could speak to Susan. Quickly thinking, I told Susan to hold the phone to my sister's ear as the doctor inserted the feeding tube. I spoke to Angela over the phone giving her instructions on how to breathe and relax. Susan said Angela was nodding her head while listening to me. Thankfully the feeding tube was placed successfully. I decided to drive back to the city the next day.

The following morning, I received another phone call from the nurse. My sister needed me to come to the hospital immediately. She was coughing up a lot of fresh blood. I ran up to the subway anxiously trying to get to the hospital. As soon as I stepped into the ICU, I could see that she was in distress. She said it felt like an elephant was sitting on her chest and could not breathe even with the ventilator machine breathing for her. The pressure she felt was like being crushed under a collapsed building. At her bedside, the doctor placed a scope down her throat to visualize the tumor. He informed us that they needed to perform emergency surgery. The tumor was compressing and obstructing her airway even more than before. They needed to put a stent in her chest to relieve the pressure.

The surgery was risky because she was on blood thinners to prevent any further blood clots. We had no choice because the surgery had to be done. She was frightened and asked the doctor if I could stay with her during the surgery. She told him that I work at a hospital. To my surprise, the doctor said I could go into the operating room with her but had to leave once she was under anesthesia. Transport arrived quickly. I was running along the side of the bed as they maneuvered her bed and equipment through the halls, around the turns, and into the elevators. They were moving fast as they pushed her bed through double doors of the operating room.

A nurse jumped in front of me and said, "Whoa, where do you think you are going?"

At the question, my sister's eyes grew wide open filled with fear. I replied, "The doctor said I was allowed to stay with her until she went under sedation." I was not going to let my sister down. I tearfully cried, "Please! I will not get in the way and I promise I will leave once she is under anesthesia."

She took mercy on both of us and said, "Fine. Grab a cap and gown."

I quickly changed and ran down the hall looking for which operating room she was in. The surgical team struggled to move her from her bed to the operating table. I kept talking to her trying to keep her calm. They told me it was time for me to leave, so I kissed her forehead. Angela performed the sign of the cross on her chest with her mobile hand. I was in awe of her gesture of faith but had to exit the room quickly as I promised.

I sat in the waiting room for several hours waiting for the surgery to be finished. I wrote her a long letter expressing my love for her. I included all the things we could do once she got better. My plans were to take her back to Virginia and nurse her back to health. I would take her children and help her raise them. She needed to get away from her husband. But in my heart, I also knew my sister would not leave him. I would do my best to convince her once she got better. I continued to sit by myself for hours waiting for any updates on her surgery and empathizing with what Nicole experienced a few weeks before. Angela made it through another risky surgery, and I tearfully called my family members.

CHAPTER 10

Throughout the years, Nicole would confide in me from time to time. I didn't want to put Nicole in the crossfire, but I had confronted my sister a few times. I also hated when she was mad at me. I remember trying to convince her to get a divorce several years before, but she got upset with me. She asked me if she got a divorce, "Where would Tom live?"

I replied, "He is a grown man and he would have to figure that out." I told her that Tom was not her responsibility. Her responsibility was to her children. Then she stated that she did not want to be a single parent. To that, I replied, "You already are." I promised her that I would always be there for her and help her with the children. If Tom wanted to get the help he needed, then that would be a different story. We would all be supportive if that were the case, but Tom did not want any help. She told me that she tried to get him into a program in the past. I also knew that if she did go through with a divorce, Tom would likely harass her for money. He would never leave her alone unless she had no money left to take.

I spent many sleepless nights at my sister's house returning late from the hospital with my niece. I found myself crying whenever I was alone. During a hot shower, I kept asking God in my head, "Why, God? Why is this happening?" I found myself crumbled on the shower floor on my knees crying hysterically as the water washed over me. I stopped crying for a moment because I heard three simple words in my ear as clear as day, *Save the children.* A calming sensation ran through my body. I slowly stood up and replied, "Yes, I will." I told God that I will accept his call and save her children. I felt a renewed strength in me as I hurried to get dressed and headed back to the hospital.

Around eight that evening, Tom arrived at the hospital. He told me to leave because I was there all day and he offered to stay for several hours. Reluctantly I agreed. I also wanted to give him time alone with his wife. I walked down the hospital corridor where I was speaking to one of her nurses. No more than five minutes passed and out came Tom running around the corner. He bumped right into us with the intention of leaving. I questioned him, "Where are you going?" He replied, "Oh, she is asleep, so I decided it is better to let her rest." We started the walk to the subway together. I asked Tom if he drove or took the subway. He told me that he was parked just around the corner. Right after he said that, he took off running up the street leaving me behind. It was the strangest behavior I have ever seen. I thought to myself, "Well, I guess he doesn't want to give me a ride back."

The following day Tom entered my sister's hospital room as I was scratching off a lottery ticket that my friend gave her in a get well card. One ticket was a winner. Tom took the winning ticket and was about to put it in his pocket. I stopped him and said, "Excuse me but that ticket was for my sister." I snatched it out of his hand. I pretended to slide the ticket into a gift bag on the window sill. I proceeded to sit in front of the bag to block him knowing that it would drive him crazy. I was experiencing firsthand his obsessive need to get money. Once I moved away from the window, he dashed over and tried nonchalantly looking into the bag. He couldn't find the ticket though because I slid it into my pocket. I know it was childish of me, but I did not want him to have it. I later cashed it in and gave the money to Nicole to buy subway tokens.

Tom even asked Susan for money at the hospital. Angela was protesting and writing frantically in her notebook, "Do not give him any money." He hit me up for money too. He would say he needed money to buy chemicals for his pool business, but we knew the only chemical he was buying was going up his nose. Tom's visits were becoming less frequent and shorter. Sadly, my sister would continue to ask me where he was and when he was coming. In the beginning, I would tell her that he was probably at work. As the weeks passed, I had to be honest with her. When she would ask, "When is he coming?" I would simply reply, "I don't know."

Nicole mentioned to me that on the night of the stroke, her mother instructed her to go to the bank and withdraw all the money. At this point in my sister's marriage, Tom did not have access to their bank account or credit cards. Angela gave Nicole the passwords to her account so that Nicole could take care of the household bills. I told Nicole that she needed to be her power of attorney. This way Nicole would be legally able to withdraw money. It was uncomfortable for us to have this discussion with my sister. Later in the day we decided to speak with her together and my sister graciously was willing to sign.

The hospital drew up a living will for my sister the night of the stroke. Her husband's name was the contact person who would make her medical decisions if she was unable to. I asked Angela if she wanted my name on the living will instead of Tom. I didn't trust Tom to have her best interest at heart. She said to leave his name on it but also to add my name as the second contact person in the event he could not be reached.

Nicole continued to work long hours at her job. She would come to the hospital after work or before depending on her schedule. She was running the household, cooking, cleaning, shopping, and taking care of her twelve-year-old brother. The end to my ten-day vacation was drawing near, but I could not bear leaving my sister. I had to let my office manager know what was going on. I had one more week of vacation time, so I decided to stay in New York. My husband returned to Virginia with the twins.

I would sleep over at my friend or sister's house. I stopped staying at my mother's house because it was too stressful, and it was putting a strain on our relationship.

She would get annoyed with me and asked me in a bitter tone, "Why do you have to stay at the hospital all day?"

I replied, "Because Angela cannot speak and needs an advocate."

She told me that was what the nurses were there for. She just didn't get it.

I snapped back, "I stay there because she is dying!"

I felt terrible once the words flew out of my mouth. I hated fighting with her. I knew she was tired and upset, but I don't think she fully understood the severity of my sister's diagnosis. I tried to explain it to her, but she replied, "They can just give her radiation like your father had when he had cancer."

My father had throat cancer that spread to his lung. Even though his determination was amazing in fighting his cancer, sadly he died three years after his diagnosis. I solemnly said to her, "Well, you see how well that worked out for him."

My sister ended up contracting a MRSA (Staph) infection, which is common when a patient is in the hospital for an extended time. Upon entering her room, we had to put on a protective gown, cap and gloves because MRSA is highly contagious. There was a small room adjacent where we put on protective gear before we could enter her room.

I knew all of my sister's nurses and had developed relationships with them. Three nurses came and squeezed into the small room with me. Panic overtook me and I questioned them, "Is everything okay?" One nurse replied that she brought her pastor friend to speak to me. I exhaled and said, "Oh, that is so nice of you. We can all pray for my sister."

The pastor introduced herself and said to me, "I am not here for your sister, because she will be fine."

I rebutted raising my voice, "Fine? Fine? How can you say that? Just look at her!" I then pointed to my sister through the glass window of her room where she was lying hooked up to all the machines. I cried out, "Don't you see what condition she is in?"

The pastor calmly responded, "Your sister will be all right."

The nurse turned to me and told me that she asked the pastor to come because all of the nurses were concerned about me. I was there every day for at least ten to twelve hours at a stretch. The nurses could see the mental and physical exhaustion toll it had taken on me.

I was silent for a moment trying to process their thoughtful concern for me. Tears welled up in my eyes touched by their compassion.

The weekend was usually the time when most family members would visit. I arrived at the hospital and proceeded to put on my protective gear. I could see about five visitors already in her room. Tom's sister Donna was there. Angela had a close bond with her. The two of them had tried to get help for Tom many times over the years. Tom arrived dashing right by me and went straight into her ICU room without putting on his protective gown. I heard Donna ask him in front of everyone, "Where have you been the last few days?" She demanded him to answer, "Angela has been asking for you." I was bending over putting on my protective shoe covers and jerked my head up when I heard screaming from her room.

Tom went ballistic yelling at his sister Donna. He was scream-ing back at her, "I am here every damn day of the week. I work full time and I still get here and spend hours with her! I have to take care of everything. You have a lot of nerve asking me anything!" His tem-per was frightening.

I hurried to get in there to try to diffuse the situation before security was called. I stood by Tom turning to him to tell him to be quiet. We are in the hospital and he cannot act like this. My sister was clearly upset watching the scene unfold in front of her.

Donna said to him, "You better stop yelling. Can't you see how upset she is getting?" She pointed to my sister, which really set him off.

He yelled even louder at Donna, "Just shut up! Don't tell me how to run my life because your life is a mess!" He slammed his hand on the glass wall and stormed out of the room.

I was shaken by his outburst. I was shocked to hear such hateful words come from him. After he left, there was an awkward silence in the room. I tried to comfort Donna and my sister. Donna said, "I am done with him," and she left the room to compose herself. I immediately changed the conversation. Then I went about my daily nursing duties to try to make my sister as comfortable as I could. Witnessing Tom's behavior did bring some insight. He becomes frightfully intimidating when confronted, and then he will cause a commotion to distract attention off him and onto someone else.

I had come to the reality that my sister was never leaving the hospital. Other family members were still optimistic. Angela continued to endure the radiation treatment, but her body was too weak from the stroke. It was obvious that there would not even be enough time for the radiation treatment to work. The lymph nodes continued to cause compression and swelling to her neck and face. The doctors still were ordering tests to continue to stage her cancer. I questioned her doctor, "Does it really matter which stage the cancer is?"

A neck vascular ultrasound was performed to check her circulation. The ultrasound technician could barely get an image because of the swelling. She was very abrupt and getting frustrated as she continued to dig the probe deeper into my sister's tender neck. My sister was mouthing the words, "Ouch, ouch." Clearly I could see the pain on her face. I told the technician to lighten up. She snapped back at me that she cannot see a clear image. Then she deliberately dug the probe deeper and harder into her swollen neck. I demanded that she stop the exam. She was torturing my sister. She told me she was not finished. I told her, "Yes, you are. You can state the exam was limited and inconclusive."

Her oncologist was forthcoming and honest with me. He said that they were still trying to stage her cancer to determine whether the lung cancer was Stage 3 or Stage 4. He explained again that radiation was the only chance she had to shrink the tumor, but her odds were not good. I replied, "But she is a young lady with a strong will to fight." He told me that her body was severely damaged from the stroke. The recovery from the stroke alone would be an uphill battle even for a healthy person. In addition to the stroke, she had a large tumor and her body had become more weakened being in bed for weeks already. He said that the only true cure for cancer is to cut it out and her tumor was inoperable.

I asked him the next obvious question, "How long does she have to live?"

He replied gently, "It could be hours to a few days to a few weeks at most."

I told him that I understood but my family was still so optimistic. I asked him, "What should I do?" He told me to set up a family meeting with her doctors that evening.

* * * * *

I was rounding the corner of the hallway right before the meeting and bumped smack into Nicole. She looked at me and saw my facial expression. She gasped, "What happened? Did she die?"

I hugged her tightly and replied, "No, but the doctors are here to speak to you and the rest of the family."

I decided not to join them in the meeting. I wanted to stay with my sister instead. After the meeting, the whole family returned to her room. All fifteen of us all dressed in our yellow gowns circled her bed. I arranged for a priest to attend, and we all held hands as we said the Our Father prayer together. The priest said an additional prayer and performed the last rites over my sister.

I cried out to the priest, "Why is this happening to us? We are a good family and we love her so much."

He solemnly replied, "I don't know."

I slowly lifted my head with my eyes piercing at Tom knowing in my heart all the stress he caused was what put her here. I refused to leave her alone that night and slept in the chair next to her.

I was trying to decide what I should do next. I was contemplating on taking a family leave of absence from my job. I would not leave her without an advocate at her side. Another consideration would be Nicole taking a leave of absence enabling her to stay with her mother. I would go back to Virginia to be with my children and take my nephew back with me. This way Nicole and her sister could take turns doing hospital shifts without the responsibility of caring for their brother. Tommy would be able to spend time with the twins.

When I did take Tommy to visit his mother in the hospital, he would stand there in a daze. I tried to encourage him that it was okay to hug her. Honestly, I did not know how much he understood. I do know that he found out that his mother was dying because he overheard a conversation in the waiting room. He was very upset because no one was telling him anything. Nicole and I agreed that I would return home with Tommy and she would take a leave of absence.

The following morning Nicole arrived at the hospital visually upset. She told me that she could not take a leave of absence from her job. She said that she told her father last night that she planned on taking a leave of absence from her job to be with her mother. He got really angry at her. He told her that she was not allowed to leave her job and that she needed to continue to work. He wanted her to work to continue paying for all the household bills.

I told Nicole it was all right if she did not want to take a leave from her job and that I would take a leave from my job. I also told her that the choice was hers alone and not up to her father. I explained to her that she was an adult and he had no control over this decision. The oncologist was in the room examining Angela. I ran into the room and I explained the situation to him. I asked him if he would speak to my niece. I wanted her to hear what he told me the day before. He kindly agreed and came outside to speak to her. He told Nicole, "Your aunt is right. You should take a leave of absence from your job and be with your mother. Do not listen to your father because your mother is not going to be alive very much longer."

I hated to be the force of reality. It broke my heart. I then stated, "I know the staging of her cancer really doesn't matter because that is not what she will die from." I asked him, "She will die from her other organs shutting down from multiorgan failure, right?" His response was yes.

As much as I did not want to leave my sister knowing that I may never see her alive again, I also knew the remaining time was for my nieces to be with their mother. I left a few days later. I kissed and hugged her goodbye. I told her that I loved her and she told me that she loved me too. She didn't fully understand that I was leaving because the next day, she asked where I was. When I heard that, I started crying hysterically again.

I stayed in touch with the nurses and doctors daily. I would get updates from my nieces on the hour. I dreaded going to work but I did. My husband worked in the evenings. He would plan fun activities for the kids to enjoy during the day. Returning home from work, I tried to spend time with them but I was too drained. I attempted to speak to my nephew about his mother's condition. I drew pictures to explain the anatomy and how the tumor was hurting her. Tommy was twelve years old at the time but was very distant and hard to reach. He only came out of his shell around the twins and seemed to have fun with them. It was hard to tell if he was in denial or just did not comprehend. Perhaps it was a combination of both. I made a video of the three boys that Nicole played for Angela. Nicole would also put the phone to her ear so she could hear our voices telling her how much we miss and love her.

CHAPTER 11

With each passing day, there were no signs of her health improving, only deterioration. I would get urgent phone calls from the hospital. They could not reach her husband regarding life-threatening medical decisions. I was the second contact on her health care proxy. Tom would never pick up his phone when the hospital called. They needed permission to start her on dialysis because her kidneys were shutting down.

After I left New York, there was another family meeting with the doctors to discuss her care. The discussion of dialysis came up. Nicole questioned doing dialysis because she knew Angela's body was shutting down. Why torture her more? She got pushback from other family members. Her aunt Donna told her that if she didn't try everything, she would regret it. Nicole and I were on the same page. We felt it was prolonging the inevitable.

The following week while I was at a doctor's visit, I received a phone call from my sister's doctor. Her doctor told me that he could not reach Tom and wanted permission for the dialysis. I told him yes only because that was what the family wanted. The dialysis was attempted as my poor mother walked into Angela's room during this process. She almost fainted when she saw the massive amount of her daughter's blood sprayed everywhere around the room. They continued to stab the catheter into her collapsed veins but ultimately, they were unsuccessful.

Her doctors wanted Tom to sign the DNR (Do Not Resuscitate) form. I felt Tom wanted to keep her alive no matter what condition she was in. This way he could continue receiving her paychecks. I pushed Nicole as well to try to convince her father to sign the DNR. She brought the subject up to him but was nervous about his reaction. He told her that he would never sign and that she doesn't know how hard this has been for him. She replied, "But what about how hard this is for her?"

I received another phone call early in the morning from the hospital. The doctor told me that they had to do an emergency electrocardioversion because her heart stopped. He said it was a very painful procedure for my sister. It was the only way to bring her heart back into normal cardiac rhythm. He told me that they could not reach her husband by phone again. I immediately called Nicole. She told me Tom's behavior had gotten even worse after I left. He was barely home. If he did come home, he was in bad shape.

With each phone call came more disturbing news. Nicole told me that Angela's left hand had turned black due to poor circulation. The doctors wanted to amputate her hand. Two days prior, she was still writing and conscious, but now she was unresponsive. I knew it was time to go back. I booked a flight for both myself and my nephew. I had been praying daily to God to please wait for me to get back to New York before she passed. I wanted to be there with her when she died. But I also told God I understood if he needed to take her sooner. I would not be upset as long as she went peacefully. I did not want her to suffer any longer waiting for me. I told a coworker as tears rolled down my face that I was flying to New York tonight but I don't think I will be back next week.

I hurried home to pack. My phone rang and I answered it immediately. The call was from Angela's nurse. I had been begging him all week to do whatever he had to do to persuade Tom to sign the DNR. He promised me he would do his best but Tom hardly came to the hospital. I held my breath waiting to hear that my sister had passed, but instead the nurse's voice sounded excited. He said, "He did it!" He finally convinced Tom to sign the DNR. I collapsed on the floor and could not believe what I just heard. I was so grateful and thanked him. A huge wave of relief washed over me, and I exhaled as if I had been holding my breath for weeks. The relief was only brief. Soon I would be boarding a plane with her son knowing his mother was not going to live much longer.

It was so hard to look at my nephew on the airplane. I kept thinking about what the next few days would bring. I glanced over at him as he was watching the TV monitor in front of him and his eyes kept twitching nonstop. I was wondering if that was just a nervous twitch. When Tommy was younger, he would run away from my husband as soon as he said hello to him and avoid making eye contact. My nephew was the youngest child with a big age gap between his sisters. I know he was coddled by Angela and his grandmother. His grandmother would even cut up his food for dinner, which I thought was outrageous. I started to believe that perhaps his excessive video game playing was his escape from the chaos that was going on. It may have been his coping method of dealing or not dealing with the tension in the house. When Tommy did speak to an adult, his voice was barely audible.

I remembered a time at my sister's house when I heard this high-pitched screaming coming from the living room. I ran into the room and saw Tom was just lying on the couch with my nephew standing there screaming for no obvious reason. I asked Tommy, "What's wrong?" He did not answer. I ran back into the kitchen and my sister said nonchalantly, "Oh, he does that all the time."

When Tommy was in sixth grade, his teacher scheduled a parent-teacher meeting to discuss Tommy's behavior. My sister took offense. She told the teacher that her son was just shy. Tommy may be shy but there was more to it. I think my sister was in denial and just could not handle anything else being out of control. I believe that there were other underlying issues with him in addition to the stress that he had been living with.

The plane finally landed. My brother was kind enough to pick us up from the airport and drive us to my sister's house. We dropped off my nephew. It was very late in the evening as we drove to my mother's house. My mother came out of the house and stood on the porch. I was insisting on going to the hospital. I told my brother that

I can take a taxi there. My mother was getting annoyed with me. I was still sitting in my brother's car as we had a shouting match from the car to the porch. I told her that Angela was waiting for me. My mother yelled back at me that Angela can wait a few more hours until the morning. We argued a bit more until I decided to go into the house. I knew we were all exhausted at this point. We tend to take out our stress easily on those we love the most. I went inside and hugged her.

I headed upstairs into our childhood bedroom that I shared with my sisters. I took down the family photo albums looking at all the captured precious memories of our past. I continued to cry as my mother entered the room. The tone of her voice had softened now and she asked me, "Why are you doing this to yourself?" She told me to try to get a few hours of sleep and head to the hospital in the morning. I knew she was right. I slept restlessly for a few hours crying myself to sleep and woke up early to head to the hospital.

As soon as I got to her hospital floor, her doctor saw me and asked, "Did you get my message?" I did not check to see if I had any phone messages but just came over to the hospital. She touched my arm and warned me that my sister was not doing well, which I knew was an understatement. Nothing could prepare me for the state that she was now in. As I entered her room, I let out a gasp. It was painful to see her several weeks ago, but now she was in worse condition. Her left hand was completely black. Her eyes were taped closed and covered with protective goggles because she had stopped producing any tears. Her face and neck were more swollen than when I last saw her. I asked the doctor if she could please remove the tape and take the goggles off. When she did, I could see that her eyes were in a fixed position. The doctor quietly turned and left us alone.

I quickly covered her hand with the blanket and sat beside her on her bed. I started combing and playing with her hair. Angela always enjoyed when I played with her hair. She was such a studious intelligent child determined to get straight A's. We had a folding table in the middle of our bedroom where she sat for hours studying. I was her little servant at that time retrieving snacks and ice tea for her. She would want me to brush and play with her hair or scratch her back as she studied. I adored her and did whatever she asked. Her friend Susan would be there studying as well. They did take breaks, which included lots of giggles and laughter that I was a part of.

I sat there crying for hours just talking to my sister as she lay still unresponsive. I asked for the priest again to give her another blessing. A sweet housekeeping lady came into the room. Once she spotted me, she nodded and performed the sign of the cross on her chest. I continued to hug my sister and promised her that I would do everything in my power to raise her son. I told her not to worry about her children and that I will handle everything. I whispered to her that she is a fierce fighter, but her body has had enough. It was time for her to go be with Dad.

I gently stroked her beautiful face and commented on all her freckles. I laid down next to her as the nurses and doctors continued to swarm in and out of the room. I spoke to her for hours reminiscing childhood memories until I felt a calming sensation come over me. I jumped off the bed and stared into her face. There was an expression in her eyes like she was experiencing a sense of awe. The doctors and nurses rushed into the room. Angela's eyes started moving, and I followed the direction of her eyes slowly scanning the room from the left to the right. I was thinking to myself she must be seeing angels in front of her. Her eyes stopped moving and landed on the clock on the wall. The doctor announced, "Time of death, 10:20." I stood still staring at the clock feeling overwhelmed because my sister's birthday is October 20th (10/20). I silently thanked God for giving me the privilege of being there with her as she entered his loving arms. I felt God's presence and the presence of many angels in the room. I realized that she spent fifty-two days in the hospital. It made me recall the night she said she saw Dad and he was with fifty-two angels. I hoped that one angel was with her for each day she endured the torture of being in the hospital.

The doctor asked me if I wanted her to call the family but I replied, "No, I will do it." I then called my niece and gave her the heartbreaking news. She in turn had to tell her sister and brother. I received a text message from my twin brother at 10:10 a.m., which is the special number we associate with my dad. October 10th was the date my father passed away. I returned his call telling him that Angela is with Dad now. He was en route to my mother's house.

Tom finally arrived at the hospital with my nieces and nephew. Nicole and I jumped into action making all the necessary phone calls to the funeral home and cemetery. The cemetery representative told us to come right away because they will be closing soon. It was a Saturday afternoon, and the cemetery was over an hour away. Tom drove us to the cemetery and I sat in the front passenger seat. Silence hung in the car. On the highway, someone in the car next to me was trying to get my attention and was pointing to our tire. We had a flat tire. Tom managed to pull off the highway and we found a mechanic. I asked if they could change the tire quickly because we were in a time crunch. It felt like we were sitting there forever.

While we were waiting, I stepped outside to call Susan and gently broke the news to her. Another forty minutes passed and I was ready to jump out of my skin. I went back to the counter and asked how much longer. Time was ticking away and we still had to drive another forty minutes to the cemetery. The man at the counter told me that they are working on it. Thirty more minutes passed and I went back to the counter. I was a wreck at this point. I said to the man, "Listen, I don't mean to be pushy but my sister who is also their mother just died. We have limited time to get to the cemetery and make her arrangements. We have been waiting here for well over an hour. Is there anything you can do to help us, please?" He was taken aback by what I said. Five minutes later we were in the car and on the road. Of course when it came time to pay for the tire, my brother-in-law used my niece's credit card to pay. I turned my head in disgust. I was stressing out on the rest of the ride, but we managed to get to the cemetery fifteen minutes before they closed.

Tom was boasting to us about how he has two deeds for a cemetery plot, one for his father and now one for Angela. I was thinking, *How insensitive is this man?* I wanted to jump across the table to choke him. I wished he was going into the plot instead of her. The manager then inquired about payment, which was usually covered by a life insurance policy. Tom proclaimed that payment would not be a problem. He said that Angela had a life insurance policy and that the money will be going directly to him. I recalled the conversation years ago when she said she took his name off her life insurance and retirement plan. The knot in my stomach twisted tighter. Doubt filled my mind because maybe his name was still on policies as the beneficiary. My eyes met with Nicole's but we kept quiet.

The next few days were a blur. My nieces and I went through the process of making all the necessary arrangements. I kept in touch with Maria who was a friend and coworker of Angela's. Angela and Maria had a close work relationship and friendship. Maria actually was the best friend of one of my college friends. My sister made that realization when she was sharing Christmas pictures. For months prior, Maria had been telling my sister about a friend of hers who was having twins and my sister had been telling Maria that her sister was also having twins. They never realized that they were talking about the same person, me. When Maria saw the photograph my sister shared with her, she proclaimed, "Oh, that's Kate and Paul! Those are my friends." Angela said through her laughter, "That's my sister, brother-in-law, and the twins!"

I would call Maria to confide in her about Tom. She too was shocked to hear about him and their marriage. Angela was always bubbly and upbeat at work, so Maria never suspected what was going on. She tearfully shared a cherished memory of throwing tiny pebbles up at my sister's office window to get her attention if Maria left work before Angela did. Angela would run to the window to look down and Maria would start waving at her and the two would break into laughter.

Angela was well loved at work, always trying to help her coworkers achieve their goals. Maria told me that many of them wanted to contribute money to help the family with the expenses. I told her that if they gave the money to Tom, he would not use it for the arrangements. She then came up with the idea to set up a college bank account for little Tommy, which her coworkers could add their gifts to. Tom would never have to find out. I mentioned what Angela said about Nicole being the beneficiary of her life insurance and retirement plan. Maria informed me that if Tom's name was taken off the plans, then he had to be aware of it. He had to be willing to sign because the law required a notarized signature since they were still married. I suspected Angela gave him an ultimatum at that time because of his gambling debts. But I wondered if Tom even remembered what he signed.

Someone handed Nicole a sympathy card after the funeral Mass. When we were all in the limousine, Tom insisted that she open it. There was a $100 bill in the card. Tom said, "I'll take that." I told him to let Nicole use that money to tip the limo drivers. I already tipped the drivers, but Tom did not know that. I just didn't want him to take the money. He reluctantly gave Nicole the card back. Later that evening, he badgered her endlessly until she gave him the money. Of course, he wasn't concerned about tipping the drivers or about repaying me. If Tom saw an opportunity where money was involved, he became obsessed to get his hands on the money and he would do anything to get it.

Nicole told me that Tom was complaining about money when we arranged for two limousines to drive the whole family to the cemetery. He said that was excessive because he only needed one and that the rest of the family could drive their own cars. I was so outraged because that was what he wanted to save money on! We were in no emotional state to drive. Unlike him, we were all distraught after the services.

Before the funeral, we sat with the funeral director to review all the arrangements, and of course the topic of payment came up. It was still a sticky situation because the life insurance had not come through yet. The director needed the signature of the beneficiary on the paperwork in order to receive payment. We still didn't know who the beneficiary was. I carefully pulled the funeral director aside without Tom watching. I quietly asked him, "What if Tom's name isn't on the life insurance as he believes but the beneficiary was my niece Nicole instead? Could she also sign the paperwork for the reimbursement?" I explained the situation to him. I also promised that I would personally pay for all the bills if for some reason the insurance did not come through. He was very sympathetic. He told me that he could see there was more than grief going on with Tom.

I slept at my sister's house that week to keep an eye on my nephew and nieces. Most of the time, I stayed in the downstairs bedroom avoiding Tom. We were still in shock. That night I was trying to sleep as I squeezed into the single bed with Nicole. Across the room, we could hear Amanda crying. Amanda always did a good job of keeping her feelings bottled up. She could not stop crying and finally cried out, "Mom loved Dad more than us." I knew how much my sister loved her children.

I softly replied, "No, Amanda. That is not true. What she did was totally wrong because she put Tom's needs before yours and that was a huge mistake."

It was so awful to hear Amanda doubt her mother's love for her, but I totally understood why she felt that way. I could not sleep as my anger grew even stronger for Tom who was the reason for all this heartache. At the same time, I was angry with my sister for allowing this to happen. I was in so much pain from losing her, and I certainly did not want to feel anger toward her. However, to hear what Amanda said tore my broken heart apart even more.

I wanted to be the one to give my sister's eulogy just like I had done for my dad. During my father's battle with his cancer, he blurted out, "Oh, Kate, I want you to give my eulogy when I pass."

I replied, "What?"

He said, "Yes, I was at a friend's funeral and his daughter gave him just a lovely eulogy. It was so special coming from a family member instead of the priest. It was very personal and that is what I want."

I responded, "Honestly, Dad, I don't think I can do that. I am not a good public speaker." I also knew that I would be a total basket case at his funeral. I loved him so much and we grew even closer during his last years.

He kept on insisting until my sister Angela chimed in. She said, "Kate, we can do it together." I reluctantly agreed.

My father was diagnosed with throat cancer and he was a true fighter. He said to me, "You know how some people would say, 'God, why me? Why, God, do I have to get cancer?'" and I nodded. He then said, "Why not me? I am not any more special than anyone else." He stated that at least he lived his life and how unfair it is for his friend's daughter who has young children to be faced with cancer. My father was only sixty-six years old at the time.

I replied to him, "Yes, that is true. But what you just said makes you very special."

My father had a strong faith, which helped him endure his treatments and surgeries. He also had a bigger-than-life personality with a crazy sense of humor. I had taken a new job at that time allowing me to drive him for his weekly chemotherapy treatments. We would find ourselves giggling over stupid nonsense and making the best of the hours during his treatments. We shared quality time sitting there just talking, and I will always treasure those memories.

My father was in the ICU because of his struggles with breathing. The patient that was in the bed across from him had been moved. My father was concerned about what happened to him and asked me to find out more information.

I said, "Dad, I don't even know the man's name."

He said, "I think they moved him to the floor below this one."

I replied, "Really, you want me to go downstairs and stick my head into every room?"

He said, "Yeah, tell him the big guy upstairs is looking for him!" Then he broke into his hearty laughter. He continued with, "Wait a minute, that doesn't sound too good."

It took a minute for me to catch on and I started laughing along with my sister. Angela's laugh was infectious. But her unique laugh usually turned into a loud honking noise. We were crying because we were laughing so much, and I was afraid that we were going to get thrown out of the ICU. After we kissed him goodbye, we got into the elevator and I pressed the number for the floor below us.

Angela said, "What are you doing?"

I said, "Well, I was going to take a quick walk around the floor and see if I could find his roommate."

Unfortunately, we did not find him, but I did learn that the patients on that floor needed less critical care, which I gladly reported back to my father.

CHAPTER 12

Nicole and I walked to our church in order to speak to the priest before Angela's funeral. We wanted to inquire about Angela's funeral Mass arrangements. Surprisingly, he was not very nice to us and reluctantly spoke with us. He told us, "Now is not the time." I was thinking to myself, *Well, when is the time?* My sister adored this priest, which Nicole and I could never understand why. As we walked home, we agreed that Angela had poor taste in men and priests.

When my father passed, it was a lot easier with his funeral arrangements. We were fortunate to have our childhood priest Father Donovan assist us. He knew my parents well because they were one of the first parishioners when the church first opened. I asked him if I was allowed to give the eulogy with my sister at my father's funeral. Angela quickly turned and said to me that she was not going to give the eulogy. I reminded her of the day when she told our dad that we would do it together. She replied, "Oh, I only said that to change the subject." The priest then went on to tell me that he would not recommend reading the eulogy at the Mass. He had witnessed grown men break down on the altar and could not finish reading their eulogy. I told him with conviction that I would not break down during the eulogy. I wanted to respect my father's wishes. It was also a great honor and the last gift I could give him.

My father also requested five songs for his funeral and he kept adding to the list. I told him that he had to limit the song choice because it was not a concert. The priest informed us that they usually have three songs during the service. I begged him to allow us to have the five chosen songs. Father Donovan was one of the nicest people I have ever met, and he allowed for this exception.

Dealing with my sister Angela's priest was a different story. He said that I could not give the eulogy at her funeral because the church did not allow it. When he explained why, I totally understood his reason. He said people would go off on tangents about their loved one and it should be about God. I asked him what if he read my eulogy first to see if it was appropriate. His answer was still no and he was not budging. Finally, he said that I could read her eulogy at the wake service the night before the funeral after he said his blessing.

I helped my nieces pick out the clothes for my sister to be buried in. We spent time deliberating choosing the songs and readings for her services. We chose one song to be played at communion, "Taste and See." My sister Debra heard that hymn during a Sunday Mass she attended while Angela was still in the hospital. I said to her that I wish Angela was able to "taste and speak" because she never was able to eat or speak a word again once she was in the hospital. Whenever we hear that song during Mass, we naturally think of Angela and our changed version of the song.

We were gathered together at the funeral home to review the readings and songs. Tom told the funeral director, "Oh, I let them pick out the readings," implying that he had made all the other arrangements. I wanted to roll my eyes but instead just kept my head down. It was unbearable for me being in the same room with him. Angela's wake services lasted for two days. When Tom managed to show up at the wake, he continued to be antsy and was pacing non-stop around the room. I was repulsed when I saw him bring his bar friends to the wake. He would stand there chatting with them and never once consoled his own children.

We arranged for a luncheon for our families between the wake services. We ended up catering lunch at my mother's house. On the drive back to the funeral home, I was bombarded with multiple text messages from my brothers, sister, and nieces. I already knew what it was about. As we drove back in separate cars, we all spotted the same thing at the same time. We all noticed the most magnificent double rainbows arching across the sky. I am a firm believer in signs and do not believe in coincidences. Those rainbows represented my sister united with my father.

The night my father died, my husband drove me back home from the hospital. As we were driving on the highway, I said to him, "I wish I had a sign from my father to show me that he was okay." As the words left my mouth, I let out a soft cry. There was a billboard ad with a light blue car that resembled my car. One word was written below the car, *Heaven*. Chills ran up and down my spine. I asked my husband, "Do you think that is a sign from my dad?" He replied, "Well, you can't get a bigger sign than a billboard."

Years later, I needed to get a breast biopsy to rule out cancer. The procedure lasted a few hours and I had to lie perfectly still in the CAT scan machine. I did my best to remain mentally calm. Toward the end of the procedure, I realized that there was soft instrumental music playing. To distract myself, I was trying to figure out which song was playing. The doctor then announced that I was all done. As I sat up, I realized what song it was and started to cry. The song was "Wind beneath My Wings." Toward the end of my father's life, he told me that he wanted that to be our song. As I listened to the soft instrumental version of the song, I felt his strong presence. I knew he was telling me that I was going to be all right.

The last night of Angela's wake, I had to muster up all my courage to stand in front of the packed room. The room was filled beyond capacity with people lining up against the walls. My heart was pounding as I nervously read her eulogy. After I finished, I looked up and saw the priest mouth the words to me, "Nice job." I hurried to sit down next to my sister Debra. She hugged me and said, "You have a gift." Those four words stayed with me only to surface again years later.

The following section is my prelude and the eulogy I wrote for my sister's wake.

Angela's Eulogy

Angela and I have been told by many people that we have the same voice, and I would like to be her voice now to express her gratitude to all of you for being here, praying for her, and being a part of her life.

Angela was such a wonderful sister who God blessed us with. Debra, Jeffrey, James, and I have only pure love for her. Growing up, our parent's primary focus was raising a close-knit, loving, caring and responsible family. Our love for each other can never be broken. This is a tribute to our special parents, Catherine and George.

Angela raised her children with those same values as it is apparent by the love and devotion she had for her children and they have for one another. She nurtured three exceptional strong and caring children, Nicole, Amanda and Tommy. She was so proud of each of them. They brought one another so much love, laughter and joy. Angela loved her husband Tom so deeply. She was a dedicated and devoted wife to him for twenty-six years.

We referred to Angela as a powerhouse because everything she did, she gave it 110 percent. Of course, the most important part of Angela's life was her family, not only her immediate family but also her in-laws were just as close to her. She loved her nieces and nephews dearly. She was always there for everyone to offer help, support and advice. She wanted everyone to succeed and be happy.

During this time, some positive things did happen—relationships with God, family members, and friends grew even deeper. New relationships developed with unbreakable bonds.

Angela often felt like she carried the weight of the world on her shoulders. She did find it difficult to rest and relax. Now she is no longer suffering and is at peace in heaven with our dad and all the others who went before her. We are the ones who will continue to suffer the loss of her not physically being with us. Angela is a part of our hearts and will always be with us. She would want us to continue living and to be happy.

My relationship with my sister was so close and strong. I am honored to be her sister. She was more than a sister and friend to me. She was part of my heart and soul. God allowed me the privilege to be there with her during her final moments and that was a gift I will be forever grateful for.

I received a message from my dad during this time that we should live by in honor of Angela, "Love all whom you hold dear. Precious is the time we share. Do not wait for tomorrow, for tomorrow may not be."

The funeral was scheduled for the next day. After completion of the Mass and cemetery services, Nicole and I arranged for a luncheon at a restaurant. There was traffic on the ride back from the cemetery. I was seated across the limousine from Tom who was clearly getting agitated. He was complaining about the traffic and expressing concern about his friends waiting for him outside of the restaurant. The luncheon was intended for family and close friends who attended her funeral. I was appalled that he invited his bar friends and his girlfriend! I could not believe my ears. Here this man had not shown a drop of compassion for his own children but was worried about his loser friends. He even yelled at his son Tommy to stop crying. I had to really push down my anger because I wanted to spit in his face.

Thankfully there was a dividing wall at the restaurant allowing me to sit on the opposite side away from Tom. I had an empty chair next to me, and my friend Helen went to sit down. I stopped her and I said, "Oh, don't sit there. That chair is for Angela." A disturbed look appeared on her face as her eyes widened. She thought I was holding the chair for my sister Angela, when in reality I was holding the chair for my friend Angela. I could not help but laugh at the expression on her face.

Tom sat with his buddies and his family members at their own table. He was bragging to his friends about how much money he was going to get from Angela's life insurance. Tom's mother was disgusted when she realized that his girlfriend was seated right next to him. Tom also declared that this was the happiest he has been in his life. Tom insensitively told Nicole that since they did not have her graduation party as her mother was in the hospital, then this luncheon could be her party as well. When she told me what he said, I was appalled. I wondered, *What the hell is wrong with him?* His remarks were just cruel.

The next morning, I had a flight scheduled to return home. I was nervous and extremely anxious to leave my nieces and nephew alone with their father. I was so scared for their safety because Tom may owe money for his drugs and gambling. Who knew what would happen now that my sister was gone?

I was with my niece until the last minute before I had to leave. On the porch, we were crying and I hugged her goodbye. Nicole said, "Wait! Don't leave yet! I see the mailman." She ran down the steps to retrieve the mail. We couldn't believe it, but there was an envelope from the insurance company. We hurried around the block to keep out of sight from Tom. Her hands were shaking as she nervously opened the envelope. This was the moment of truth. Did Angela truly change the beneficiary on her policy? Nicole read the letter and announced that she was indeed the sole beneficiary of her life insurance. Tom would not be getting the money he was bragging about. Nicole, having witnessed her father's uncontrollable temper, was terrified to tell him about the insurance. I told her not to say a word for now. He will eventually find out on his own and to just hide the letter. The letter was hers and addressed to her, not him. It was such a relief knowing that at least the money will be secure. The money would cover the funeral expenses and the rest used for the benefit of her children. Nicole was mature beyond her years and trustworthy. There was no doubt that she would always use the money to take care of her siblings.

My next focus was on how to get custody of my nephew Tommy. I had to keep up the appearance that I was still friends with Tom to stay on his good side. I was thinking about what would be the best way to persuade him to let my nephew live with me. I believe Tom was delusional. In his mind, he felt he did nothing wrong and nothing was ever his fault. He was always the victim. Nicole would sneak a look at her dad's phone when he was passed out on the couch. She read in text messages in which he expressed how he was suffering because he had to take care of his wife who was in the hospital and his mother who was suffering from Alzheimer's. He complained how everything fell solely on his shoulders. I had to play into his narcissistic mindset and approach him carefully. I decided to write a letter as my first attempt allowing the seed to be planted.

Dear Tom,

I know everyone's life has changed and we are all suffering the devastating loss of Angela. I am most concerned about little Tommy because he is just a child and was so close to her. Being a single parent with sole responsibility of a child is very challenging. Nicole and Amanda are adults now with their own lives with work and school. They are at an age where they would want to move on with their lives and maybe get married and start their own family.

I spoke to Angela when she was in the ICU and she wanted little Tommy to live with me. I know this is a difficult decision, but I feel it would be best for him. I want to help you and him. He would be well taken care of. He could go to school with the twins. I will help him with his homework and school projects. Paul is here after school every day, and I get home by five o'clock and one thirty on Fridays. Someone is home twenty-four hours a day to care for him. He will have his own room and home-cooked meals. He will have the twins to play with, and we could get him involved in extra-school activities. We will get him counseling for coping with the loss of his mother. We will get him to school daily and take care of any medical, dental and eye care.

I know this is a huge decision for you right now, but it would be good for little Tommy. He is at a critical age in his life. I hope we can work together to do this quickly, easily, and with the least amount of stress for little Tommy. You know how much I love Angela, and I want to honor her wish. I love all of your children so much, and I want to help. I will be up in New York soon, and we can discuss it then or you can call me anytime.

Love,
Kate

CHAPTER 13

The first Monday back at work was the hardest. It took all my strength to drive to work and open the door to my office. I was sick to my stomach and wanted to vomit. I did not want to encounter coworkers expressing their condolences. I could barely keep it together. The day dragged on slowly as well as the weeks. I would cry driving to work and during lunch and resume crying on my drive back home. I alienated myself as much as I could from everyone. As soon as I arrived home, I would curl up on the couch and continue to cry. I barely ate or slept. My phone sat next to my bed just in case my nieces called. I made them promise to call me any time day or night if they needed me.

Tom never responded to my letter, so I decided to reach out again to him. I asked him if he wanted Tommy to stay with us before school started up again. He was hesitant but then he said, "If Tommy wants to go live with you, then I'll let him. It is up to him." I was so thrilled but also thought that it was odd for Tom to leave the decision up to his twelve-year-old son.

I knew Tom did not want the pressure of being a parent although Nicole was the one acting like the parent. Tom continued to go out every night partying because now he was able to cash in my nephew's social security money. The money was intended for the welfare of his child, but that did not matter to him. Tom continued not to work while Nicole took care of the house and her brother. She even had to walk to the grocery store and lug the groceries back home in her arms because Tom would not let her use the car.

I could not contain my excitement that Tom may allow Tommy to live with me. I desperately needed to share the good news with someone, so I decided to tell a coworker friend of mine. No less than ten minutes later, I received a text message from Nicole. My elation vanished when I read Nicole's message. Tom changed his mind even though Tommy said that he wanted to live with me. Tom told Tommy that if he left, it would screw up the social security money. He bribed Tommy to stay in New York with a promise to buy him a new video gaming system.

I could not hold back my tears and my coworker asked, "What is wrong?" I told her and ran outside. I needed a minute alone to compose myself. As I returned rounding the corner, I heard her say to another coworker how annoying I was and how she was tired of hearing me talk about my brother-in-law and those children. I almost fell against the wall when I heard her. I thought she was a good friend and it was so hurtful to hear her say that.

Every day continued to be mental hell for me. I was stripped away from any normal grieving process. I had no choice but to wait to see if Tom would step up as a parent, and the waiting was agonizing. It felt like my other family members did not fully comprehend the impending danger the children could face with Tom's unsupervised behavior. This tension was putting a strain on my relationship with my husband, family and friends.

Every emotion would course through my veins. I felt overwhelmed with grief, anger, anxiety and fear. My hatred for my brother-in-law grew stronger with each of my niece's updates on her father. I was so angry at him as well as my sister for putting up with all his crap. I would feel guilty because I still never wanted to feel anger toward her. She suffered so much undeserved pain the last few months of her life as well as the pain she endured living with her husband. Toward the end of her life, she did stop asking where Tom was. I know she loved him, but she did not get his love back in return.

That evening, Nicole informed me again that Tom was out all night. I was so mad and I stomped downstairs to tell my husband.

He said, "What can you do? He is a grown man and you cannot control his actions. Maybe Angela had a bit of a handle on him, but now he is free to do whatever he wants." I just wanted to scream at the top of my lungs as I stormed back upstairs. Tom continued to go out enjoying himself with no regard for his children who were home suffering. It was so unfair that Angela had to die and Tom continued to live his reckless life.

I was pacing the floor of my bedroom feeling the stream rise off me from my anger. Out of nowhere, a revelation popped into my mind. Perhaps Tom wasn't enjoying our suffering because he has no concern about our feelings at all. I thought maybe he was a true sociopath. His narcissistic behavior fit the bill. He can be very charming when he wants to be. He is intelligent and self-centered with a conniving manipulative disposition. Tom may not be enjoying our suffering because he only thinks of himself. But there is one who is deeply enjoying our suffering, one who will try to creep into my mind and would love to take hold of me in my most vulnerable state. Out of my mouth, I loudly stated, "Satan, go away. I know that you are very powerful. Tom may have let you into his soul, but God is even more powerful." It was at that moment I realized that I was indeed in such a fragile state of mind, but I was determined to take back control. I decided I was not giving any more power to Tom or to Satan. God called me to save the children and that was what I was going to do. I knew I had no control over Tom but only how I responded to him.

The next morning, I called Amanda and asked if she would testify in court about her father's behavior. She replied, "I can't, Aunt Kate. He is my dad." I knew not to press her and more time needed to pass. I decided to use the time to do my research. It was uncomfortable to make numerous phone calls to lawyers in Virginia and New York. I was on a fact-finding mission to find out what was involved in order to obtain custody through the legal channels. I found out what documentation was necessary to enroll little Tommy into the Virginia school system. I needed his birth certificate and social security card, which Nicole sent to me.

I called everyone under the sun covering all the bases if the time ever came. I needed to obtain his vaccination history, which I did not have access to. I called the pediatrician's office. The receptionist remembered my sister. She told me how she really liked Angela and was sorry for my loss. I explained the situation and she said she will try to do what she can. I called the church for his Baptism certificate leaving no stone unturned. One week later, I received all the documents in the mail.

Day after day, nothing changed. I don't know how I drove home from work through my endless crying. My car became my safe haven. I would find myself screaming out loud in frustration to God and my sister for help. Through my tears, I came across a radio station playing contemporary Christian music. The music began to soothe me with the encouraging positive lyrics. The songs felt like a direct message from God. I connected with the music having faith in the wisdom from the lyrics.

I knew family members and some of my friends were deeply concerned about my fragile state of mind and well-being. They felt helpless not knowing how to console me. However most phone calls were focused on getting the dirt on Tom. I am sure it is human nature, but it got under my skin. No one ever mentioned my sister's name as if she were forgotten. Tom was the highlight. It made me even angrier if that were possible. I would lose my temper when I heard a comment like, "Oh, if we only knew what Angela wanted for her son." I knew what she wanted because she told me and she wrote it down!

When a friend called to check up on me, she could hear the distress in my voice. She decided to book a flight with her husband to visit me the following week. My husband Paul commented that this was the first time he caught a glimpse of "me" returning to life in their company.

I knew I was withdrawing and was on edge when I spoke to anyone. My mother commented how wonderful it was when she heard the old me in my voice after I delivered some good news regarding my nephew. She was so delighted and relieved. I didn't have the heart to call her back minutes later when the good news quickly turned into bad news. I made a conscious decision to limit phone calls to my family and friends.

I called an acquaintance for legal advice regarding obtaining custody of my nephew. He asked, "Why would you want to take him away from his only parent?" I informed him of Tom's chronic drug use and his gambling addiction. I told him how Angela wanted me to raise her son. At the end of our conversation, he informed me that the court would never grant me custody if Tom was alive.

CHAPTER 14

I knew I was building a wall around myself, keeping everyone at a distance. I found some comfort at church when I attended alone. It never failed that I would end up crying during the Mass at some point. In the church bulletin, I read about a Centering Prayer workshop being offered. The description seemed like it may be a good fit for me. Centering Prayer is an ancient prayer practice that simply involves sitting in silence with God. The bulletin stated Centering Prayer is a therapeutic prayer, which I was in desperate need of. I decided to sign up for the workshop. The workshop was followed by six weeks of Centering Prayer information sessions to explore more deeply the prayer practice and our experiences with it.

I found Centering Prayer was a beautiful way to pray. The intention of the prayer is to just sit silently with God. Centering Prayer is not magic, but it has a mystical quality in the sense that you feel spiritually connected to God's love. The guidelines I learned for Centering Prayer Practice start with choosing a sacred word. The word is intended to bring your mind back into the silence. The moment I began the prayer, many thoughts wildly ran through my mind. I ever so gently used my sacred words, *be still*. Do not fight distractions as they continue to emerge; just use your sacred word. Sit comfortably with your feet on the ground, hands open on your lap, and eyes closed. It may be helpful to take several deep breaths to slowly release any stress. At the end of the twenty-minute session, remain in silence with your eyes closed. Slowly say the Our Father Prayer out loud.[1] The prayer has a profound transforming effect, allowing God's love in and in turn allowing his love to work through you.

Centering Prayer emotionally calmed me and I always felt better after our group met. During the prayer, I could feel warm tears roll down my cheek, and I knew it was the start of my healing process. All I wanted was peace in my life. I am not the type of person who thrives on drama in my life but rather craves a peaceful existence. I despised the hateful dark thoughts that passed through my mind. Centering Prayer was cleansing me of those thoughts as I grew closer to God.

Our group leader suggested several books to read. *Open Heart Open Mind* by Father Keating was the first book on Contemplative Prayer that I read. I connected with this prayer because of its simplicity and spirituality. Initially when the Centering Prayer group was formed, I felt that I didn't need a group in order to pray. However at the last information session, I felt this warm sensation in my chest when the topic of communal prayer came up, which I took as a sign to join the Centering Prayer group. What a blessing that turned out to be because I met the three amazing group leaders. My healing continued with their friendship and love over the years.

The following words from Father Keating's book helped me better understand the dynamic of group prayer. "I do not know how it works, but when a group of like-minded people committed to the transformative process are together, the force of the energy is certainly up a number of decibels higher. You do not have to do anything but sit still and let your mind be quiet. Know that God's word is spoken fully only in silence. Be still and you will know, not by the knowledge of the mind, but by the knowledge of the heart, who God is and who you are". (Thomas Keating). God is All in All.[2]

At the end of a Centering Prayer session as we were sitting in a small circle the church bells chimed in the distance. I felt the same warm sensation again in my chest, and I realized the church bells

---

[1]   Contemplative Outreach Ltd., *The Method of Centering Prayer The Prayer of Consent* (NJ, Contemplative Outreach Ltd., 2016).

[2]   Thomas Keating, O.C.S.O., *Keynote talk delivered by Fr. Thomas at the Annual Conference of Contemplative Outreach* (Snowmass, CO, 2012).

were playing the song "Taste and See." I could not stop the tears, so I decided to share with the small group about the song and my sister. I offered to bring the closing prayer for our next meeting. Instead, I felt compelled to write about what Centering Prayer meant to me.

No Words Are Needed

As I hold my child in my arms,
Our relationship and connection deepens.
No words are needed.
Safety, trust and security are felt in my loving
    arms,
Unconditional love grows with each embrace.
No words are needed.
To center is to allow myself to rest in the loving
    arms of God,
To be in the presence of the One who loves me
    the most.
No words are needed.
Just to relax and rest in his arms.
Just to be still
Just to be silent
Just to be one with God
Just as my children are at the center of my heart
    and soul,
We, as children of God, are at his center.
No words are needed.

Kate Lynn Winters

The group leader asked if I would consider submitting my prayer to the *Contemplative Outreach* Newsletter.[3] I never considered doing something like that before. I thought perhaps God wanted me to submit the prayer to reach someone else. I was starting to under-

---

[3] Contemplative Outreach, *Contemplative Outreach News* (NJ, Contemplative Outreach, 2013).

stand how the Holy Spirit moves us to help others. Centering Prayer made me more sensitive and attuned to the Holy Spirit. I submitted the prayer, and it was published in the following month's newsletter.

The church offered counseling, so I scheduled weekly appointments. The counselor was kind and really listened to me. It was refreshing to speak to someone outside of my circle. I also decided to meet with a Spiritual Director to learn what was involved. I read about it in the church bulletin and felt that familiar pull in my chest. I believed it was God nudging me to explore other opportunities.

The Spiritual Director made me realize that my anxiety cannot change the outcome. I told her about a sign I saw on my drive over that stated, "Worry is an insult to God." During our conversation, she explained how my life was in the process similar to the Paschal Mystery. The Paschal Mystery is the Catholic faith belief of the passion, death and resurrection of Christ. She told me that I was experiencing the process of transformation in my life. My old life was gone, but as I connected more spiritually with God, my new life will emerge. I struggled with letting go of my old life. I loved my life the way it was before my sister died. She further explained that I was enduring pain and suffering just as Jesus did. He felt abandoned by his friends at the end but knew God was always with him. Once Jesus accepted the fact that his old life was over, he was then able to receive his new life. She advised me to talk and pray to Jesus because we shared similar journeys.

I blurted out to her, "I am broken." Her reply was, "No, you are not. You are just wounded." She patiently listened to my weekly updates about how Tom managed to slither his way out of everything. She told me Tom was like a tornado, and I had to try to pull myself from the gripping power of this storm. She ended our session saying, "It won't last forever." I looked up at her strangely because it sounded like the words were from God instead of her. I left with a renewed confidence that there was an end in sight but knowing I still had to be patient.

Nicole was my spy in New York and kept me informed of Tom's whereabouts. His behavior was getting predictable. As soon as he cashed a social security check, he would go missing for days at a time. He blew through the money within days. I called the Social Security department to report the misuse of money but was told that there was nothing I could do unless I had proof. I then hired a private investigator to follow Tom in hopes of gaining some valuable information. I spoke with several representatives at the Child Protective Service (CPS) Agency. I was told that their hands were tied because there were other adults in the house. I then knew I had to convince my nieces to move out of their childhood home and leave their brother behind.

Nicole did her best every day to try to wake her brother up for school in the morning. Tommy would stay up late playing games on his computer and would refuse to go to school, so Tom would let him stay home. Tommy would complain that his stomach hurt. Nicole pleaded with her father that Tommy needed to see a doctor. Tom kept promising her that he would take him. Tom never took him to the doctor or for grief counseling. He just continued to ignore his children.

As the weeks passed, Tommy would wake up late in a panic because he did not want to get detention at school. He must have been getting warnings at school because of his absences. Tommy would beg Nicole to walk him to school, which was only a few blocks away. Nicole would usually walk with Tommy to school but this morning she too was running late. She told Tommy to ask their father to walk him to school. Tommy's response to her was, "He is not a real father."

I called Tommy's school and was told that a truancy advocate will be sent to the house but that never happened. I documented every time Tommy missed school. He missed over thirty-five days of school that year. Sadly, he was still promoted to the next grade. I do not know if the school sent letters about his attendance. I would assume they would have to, and I hoped they did because it would have been additional pressure on Tom. I logged every detail and became obsessive about my record-keeping in case I had to go to court. I advised Nicole as much as it pained her that she needed to step back and let Tom be the parent instead, and she agreed. She was still hopeful that Tom may do the right thing.

My nieces wanted to go out to celebrate Amanda's birthday and asked their father if he would be home that evening. He promised that he would, but he never came home. They did not want to leave their brother alone, so they decided to call their grandmother to see if she would come over. The girls went out even though they were angry at their father. Tom did not return home until the following morning. He was surprised to see his mother there when he entered the house. His hand was badly cut up and bleeding. She asked him what happened to his hand, and he replied with some ridiculous story.

Tom was well versed in his storytelling. He was notorious for causing multiple car accidents blaming the other person involved. One household chore Tom had was grocery shopping. Many times he would arrive home empty-handed and tell my sister a tale about how he bought the groceries but they were stolen from the car. She called me naturally upset, and I told her it sounded like nonsense to me.

Another memory I had of Tom was when he picked up Tommy after he spent the day with the twins. I gave Tom a book Angela wanted to read. Inside the book, I placed an envelope for his mother containing money as a thank-you gift. His mother would babysit my twins and became like another grandmother to them. I decided to call my sister to make sure she got the book. Lo and behold, the envelope was missing. Tom said it fell out of the car. I was so angry, thinking, *How can he steal from me and his own mother?* We were the two people in his life who were constantly helping out with his children.

The stress and pressure continued to mount as weeks turned into months. I would advise my nieces on next steps, not really knowing what the outcome would bring. They put their trust in me and knew I had their best interest at heart. The stakes were high if I made a wrong decision. I wished I was living in New York, but at the same time, it was better that I didn't. If I were still in New York, Tom would want to constantly drop Tommy off at my house knowing I would watch him. Nothing would have changed. I also knew my obsession would lead me to follow Tom around, and I would be the one with a restraining order against me.

Nicole's birthday came without any acknowledgment from her father. He didn't bother to say happy birthday, but instead he hit her up for money. He also found out through family gossip that he was not getting Angela's life insurance money and was furious. He had a confrontation with Nicole that evening and then he stormed out of the house.

I had a flight booked to New York on October 10 to honor the tenth anniversary of my father's passing. The trip was intended for a family reunion with a visit to the cemetery. I was dreading the trip but I couldn't wait to see my nieces and nephew. The mere thought of entering the house without my sister there made my skin crawl. As I walked through the door, I could feel a dark heavy presence in the air, which made me physically sick. That feeling lingered with me for weeks. I had to try to focus because I wanted to get my hands on my sister's notebooks from the hospital. I needed to find the notebook in which she wrote that she wanted me and my husband to raise her son. I thought that could be used as proof in court.

As I looked through her notebooks, many sad memories filled me. Tom stood a few feet in front of me and Nicole watching. Then he reprimanded us, "You two better not be getting a headstone. I have a friend who can get one for a good deal." Translation: Tom would lie about buying a headstone and pocket the cash. Tom always has a friend for everything. I told him that we were going to the cemetery to meet up with the family for a memorial for my father. That was the truth, well, at least part of the truth.

Our original plan was to buy a headstone for Angela and to meet up with the family. Nicole said that she wanted to give Tom two months to see if he actually would buy one. If he didn't, then she would order the one we picked out. I respected her wishes but told Nicole not to give him any money for a headstone. Needless to say, two months later, Nicole went back to purchase the headstone.

CHAPTER 15

October 20 arrived bringing added pain; it would have been my sister's fifty-second birthday.

My nephew didn't have a house key, so he sat on the porch for hours after school. Tom was not home as he usually was in the afternoon. Little Tommy had to wait until Nicole came home from work later that evening to get inside the house. He did walk about a mile to Amanda's job but she was not there. A coworker recognized Tommy. She also knew Nicole, so she called her. Nicole immediately called her father to tell him that Tommy was locked out of the house. Tom said he was at work and could not leave. Tom never made it home that evening and did not return home until two days later.

I asked Tom if he would let Tommy visit us during the fall break from school. He agreed but I had to pay for his plane ticket and make all the arrangements. I wanted Tommy to spend some time with the twins, and I desperately wanted to see him. We enjoyed family fun activities for Halloween going to a corn maze and carving pumpkins. I attempted to speak to him to see how he was feeling. He could barely make eye contact with me and mumbled his responses in his low voice. I did not press him. He spent the rest of the time with his cousins with whom he felt comfortable.

Having Tommy stay with us allowed some free time for my nieces to enjoy their annual Halloween party. They were actually looking forward to the party and had fun decorating. They had accumulated a variety of decorations over the years. Nicole arrived home that evening and was shocked to see Tom's girlfriend sitting on the couch. He introduced her, but they did not stay long.

Nicole called me hysterically crying. She was so upset because not only did Tom steal the alcohol she purchased for the party, but also he had stolen all of their Halloween decorations. Nicole confronted him the next day when he returned home. She yelled at him that he had no right to take her stuff. He casually said he lent them to the bar for them to use for their decorations and that he would get them back. Nicole knew that was a lie and would never happen. This was not a new habit of his, but now my sister was not there to make things right. The girls decided to cancel their party.

CHAPTER 16

T he time came for Nicole to make her escape from the house. Their homelife was not improving, and I needed to get CPS involved. It was a huge decision, which I did not take lightly. I anguished and prayed over this decision. I wished my father or sister were alive for their advice. I was worried beyond belief for Nicole's safety. She would have to deal with Tom's temper once he found out. He was not going to let her leave that easily even though she was an adult.

Nicole has always been an amazing loving person. Even when she was a baby, I knew how special she was. We shared a strong bond, and I knew she trusted me. But I did not want to be in her shoes and was praying that Tom would not hurt her. She mustered up the courage and told him that she was planning on moving out to live with a friend. His response was baffling. He told Nicole that he did not care what she did.

However, as soon as Nicole started to pack up her Precious Moment Figurines, which I had given for each birthday, Tom got agitated. He got into a fight with her and refused to let her take them. The family photo albums were off limits too. Months later, he willingly let my sister Debra borrow some photo albums when she asked. She told him she wanted to make copies of some pictures. Years later, we were able to recover the rest of the family photo albums. Unfortunately, they were covered with mold and mildew from neglect. When we opened the container to look at the albums, we were assaulted with this horrendous smell. The pages were damaged and stuck together. It was so painful when we dragged the containers to the trash. I felt like we were throwing my sister's life away instead of preserving the precious photos to cherish. Rage and sadness filled me again with a renewed disgust for my brother-in-law.

I was on my evening phone call with Nicole when she told me that Tom was out. I told her to quickly gather as much of her clothes and belongings together and just throw them into large garbage bags. This was the time for her to make her move. She hurried like a mad woman not knowing when her father would return. Her friend drove her to my mother's house where she went into hiding. It was heartbreaking for her to leave her brother and sister behind.

My anxiety heightened with concern for my other niece Amanda. She would have to deal with the aftermath from her father. Tom put pressure on Amanda to find out where Nicole was living, but Amanda would just give him the cold shoulder. Amanda was a full-time student and worked part-time. When Tom harassed her for money, she would only give him a few dollars. Tom pressured Amanda but not to the extent that he would pressure Nicole.

Tom's behavior did not change as conditions grew worse in the house. Amanda was out most of the day between work and school. It was up to Tom to take control of the household responsibilities. I could not call CPS because Amanda was still living there. I needed her to escape the same way Nicole had done. It was like instant replay. A few weeks later, I was on the phone with Amanda and she told me that Tom was out. She hurried around stuffing all her belongings into garbage bags. My nephew Tommy was naturally upset when he saw her. He started crying and pleading with her not to leave. Every time Amanda put an item into a garbage bag, Tommy would remove it. It tore at my heartstrings, and now I was questioning my decision knowing that my nephew had to have felt abandoned. However, Tommy had to remain alone under his father's care. For me, the waiting continued.

My nieces ended up getting an apartment together, which was not too close to their brother. My nephew would end up calling Nicole in a panic when he was alone at night. Nicole would send a taxi cab to pick Tommy up and bring him to her apartment. She did not own a car. Tommy was afraid to be alone in the cab but more afraid to be alone all night at the house. This occurrence usually happened around three in the morning various days of the week.

I called CPS to report that my nephew was alone at 3:00 a.m. The representative on the phone asked me his age. I explained the situation to her how Tommy was not a mature twelve-year-old and had behavioral issues. Her next question was, "Could he make a peanut butter and jelly sandwich?"

I replied, "Yes." I told her that his father would probably not come home at all and was at a bar.

She replied, "Can you prove it?" She said my nephew was old enough to be alone and he was old enough to dial 911 for help. With that, she ended the conversation.

I was so furious at her response. I called the family lawyer and told him that I wanted to proceed with going to court for custody. The truth was my nephew at that time did not have the mental capacity to call 911. Later, my nephew was questioned about what he would do if there was a fire in the house. His answer was that he would call Nicole.

Tom went missing again for another two days after the social security checks arrived. My husband told me he had heard enough. He couldn't bear to see what this was doing to me, so he called CPS. This time, they took some action. They sent someone to the house to investigate. Tom was furious, especially when they requested a urine sample for a drug screening. He called Nicole yelling at her because he believed she placed the call. The agency would not release the name of the person who called, which made Tom irate.

He screamed at Nicole, "Now look what you've done! Don't you know they will take Tommy away and put him in foster care?"

Nicole told her father that she did not make the call and knew nothing about it. Then she frantically phoned me. I tried to calm her down explaining that Tommy would never go into a foster home. I assured her the agency would reach out to a family member to take him first before placing him into a foster home. Tom then believed that his sister or my mother were behind the phone call. He was so angry at them, which I felt guilty about. I had to keep up the appearance that I was Tom's ally, keeping suspicion off me.

I was now in constant contact with the CPS personnel assigned to my nephew's case. I spoke to them on a regular basis with updates. I informed them when my nephew was left alone or missed another day of school. I felt they were sincere in trying to help, but their hands were tied. For weeks, Tom continued to dodge giving a urine sample to be tested.

The pressure was being applied to Tom. When he went missing overnight, I called to file a report. Tom told them that Tommy was not alone and his grandmother was there. I then explained that may be true; however, his grandmother is in her eighties with end-stage Alzheimer's. She needs to be under watchful supervision and certainly not capable of watching my nephew. There were numerous times when she would leave food cooking on the stove unattended and came close to setting the house on fire.

Tom would take his mother to the bank and proceed to use her ATM card to withdraw all of her money. He knew when her social security check was deposited. The bank notified Tom's sister because her name was also on the account. The bank investigation revealed that this was the second time and suggested pressing charges. Tom stealing from his mother is terrible, but I was also excited because now we had something concrete on him. This was a criminal act that he could be charged with. His mother and sister did not file charges, and once again disappointment set in. Every time we had something solid on Tom, he slithered his way out as if he was untouchable.

Tom's half brother Eric was released from jail and out on parole. He was in jail because he got into a fight and attempted to light the person on fire. Eric surfaced while my sister was in the hospital. Angela was very upset that he even came to the hospital to visit her. She made it crystal clear that he was not welcomed in their house and wanted him to be kept away from her children. Nicole confronted her father expressing her mother's concerns. Tom disregarded both of them and instead went palling around with Eric. Eric told Tom's sister that they were doing a lot of cocaine together and hanging out in bars. Eric is sleazy and would make inappropriate sexual comments in front of all the children.

Tom invited Eric to live in the house with my nephew. This was a parole violation. To make matters worse, Tom also allowed his twenty-year-old bartender girlfriend to live there. This girl had a reputation in their neighborhood for using cocaine. I immediately called CPS when I found out they were crashing there. My mind went crazy with worry not knowing how my nephew was managing. The home phone line was cut off because Tom did not pay the phone bill. Tommy would forget to charge his cell phone making conversations infrequent.

The CPS representative told me it was obvious Tom had drug and mental problems. He said the system is extremely slow and sadly children are left in much worse situations than my nephew. He told me to keep my court date, but they will continue to do what they can. There were several scheduled mandatory meetings that Tom had to attend with my nephew as their investigation continued. My nieces were at all the meetings but dreaded seeing their father. Tom would be on edge, agitated and high when he arrived. He would constantly pace around the room. He went into ranting fits yelling insults and complaints. He was verbally abusive to my nieces as well as to the CPS personnel that were present at the meeting.

CHAPTER 17

I was at an emotional breaking point. Tom continued to do whatever he wanted. It seemed to me that Tom had never been held accountable for anything in his life. Nicole shared with me a time when she was about fourteen years old when the police along with Tom's boss arrived at their house. Tom had stolen equipment and supplies from his job. My sister was at work and Tom panicked when he saw the cops at the door. He made his daughter open the door and answer them. He told Nicole to tell the police that he was not home. She was extremely nervous and uncomfortable lying for him. The police officer pressured her because they could see Tom's car in the driveway. They finally left while Tom hid the whole time.

Since we were approaching the season of Lent, I decided to attend a Lenten Retreat led by my Spiritual Director. She thought it could be beneficial for me. The retreat met weekly with assigned daily readings. We were asked to look at the picture on the cover of our weekly booklet and to imagine we were part of the scene. One image was a path that resembled a cross symbolizing that we are always approaching different paths in our lives. Will we walk with God or walk down another path away from God? My mind wandered to which path Tom would choose.

We were asked to make a quiet sacred place in our house just to be alone with our thoughts and reflections. I set up a little altar in the guest room, which I hoped soon would be Tommy's room. I closed my eyes and felt a wave of peace and serenity come over me unlike anything I have ever felt before. I found myself smiling in spite of the fact that any minute the feeling would be gone with the next urgent call from my niece regarding my brother-in-law. But for those few seconds, peace washed over me.

There were questions posed at the end of each reading. One question was, "Is there something in your life today that makes you feel alone needing God?" I journaled my answer. I wrote that I have never felt so lonely as I have these past few months and that was the driving force that brought me to the retreat. I know God is the only one who will be able to help me through this. I know I have some support from others, but they are only supporting actors. God has become my best friend. I know my pain is my own pain. God is the only one who knows how I feel every second of the day.

The following Psalms used during the retreat really resonated with me.

> To you, my God I lift up my soul
> O God within me, You I place my trust
> Let me not feel unworthy; let not fear rule over me.
> Compel me to know your ways, my God;
> Instruct me in your paths,
> Lead me in your truth, and teach me
> For through your will I will know wholeness
> You have been with me from the beginning,
> Forgive the many times I have walked away from you
> Choosing to follow my own will.
> I seek your guidance, once again. I yearn to know your peace,
> Companion me as I open to your will.
> Relieve the blocks in my heart that keep me sep-
>   arated from you;
> See all the darkness within me; fill it with your
>   healing light. (Psalm 25)[4]

---

[4] Nan C. Merrill, *Psalms for Praying* (NY, Continuum, 2002), p.54. All three Psalms were adapted by the Director of the Lenten Retreat which the author, Kate Lynn Winters, attended.

I was taken by the Psalmist stating fear hinders complete trust. I had to trust in God to heal me not knowing how it would be done. I felt shame over my past sins even though I went to confession for forgiveness. Attending the retreat was an eye-opening experience giving me a clearer perspective. I realized that God had forgiven me, yet I had not forgiven myself. Like any good parent, we forgive our children when they are truly sorry. Since God is our caring father, he does not want to see us suffer; instead, he offers forgiveness and comfort in the form of divine love. The psalm below felt like it was written directly for me.

> Awaken me, O Blessed One, with your holy mercy.
> That I might be free of fear.
> Hear my prayer, O Holy One
> Give ear to the cry of my heart.
> For anxious doubts assail me and loneliness and pain;
> I forget your gentle love of me
> So overwhelming are my fears.
> Yet, behold, you are my Helper,
> The upholder of my life.
> With you, I have the strength to face my fears;
> Your faithfulness sustains me.
> With boundless confidence, I abandon myself.
> Into your loving hands, for you deliver from my
> fears. (Psalm 54)[5]

"What healing do I need in my life today?" That was another question posed to us. I wrote that the anguish over the loss of my sister stirred up in me deep-rooted pain that I thought was resolved. I had to let God heal me if I was open to his invitation. God is gentle and non-intrusive. An upset child may lock themselves in a room. A parent's instinct is to rush in to offer comfort. However, the child may want to be alone for a while and not ready to receive comfort. God is always patiently waiting for us to open the door ever so slightly to let him in.

---

5   Merrill, pp.104–105.

I had lived in the darkness for so long but not felt a glimmer of light in my life. I was a prisoner of my pain, and my only crime was loving my sister and her children. I had to release this blanket of pain that had been suffocating me in order to move out of the darkness. It was unnerving to realize how attached I had become to my pain. I knew I would not survive in this state of mind if I remain within the darkness for much longer. As the retreat was coming to a close, the following portion of Psalm 86 was used. This touched my heart as it strengthened my spiritual journey.

> Give ear to my cry, O Comforter, and answer me
> For I am in great need of You.
> You are my God, my beloved, be gracious to me.
> Heart of my heart for you I desire to walk all day.
> Give ear to my prayer, O compassionate one.
> Listen to my heartfelt plea.
> In time of trouble, I dare to call upon you.
> For you hear the cry of those in need.
> Teach me your ways, Mighty Counselor,
> That I may walk in your truth, write my name
>   upon your heart.
> O God, numerous fears rise up within me;
> Like an army, they seek to overwhelm me and
>   keep me in darkness.
> Be present to me and receive my prayer;
> Fill me with strength and help me to release each fear.
> Pour forth your light into my soul,
> That all that is hidden in darkness may come
>   forth into awareness.
> For you, O my beloved God, are my Redeemer
> And my Comforter. (Psalm 86)[6]

The retreat ended on Easter Sunday, and I wrote this prayer.

---

[6] Merrill, pp.177–179.

For Us

Tears slowly roll down my face at the thought of
    all the physical and even more painful wounds
    of betrayal that you endured for us.
I wonder would I have just stood in the crowd or
    had the courage to step forward for you.
It's truly astounding your love and concern for us
    even during your final moments of earthly life
    shown to us in the form of forgiveness.
Lord, help me to be more attuned to the crosses
    others may carry.
Lord, guide me to practice and receive the duality
    of freedom from forgiveness.
Lord, thank you for the gifts of renewed life,
    internal peace and light that we are blessed to
    receive through your sacrifice.
Lord, may we always feel the everlasting love you
    have for us.
                  Amen.

                      Kate Lynn Winters

CHAPTER 18

I continued my spiritual journey by reading books about Contemplative Prayer. Reading distracted my mind from worry. Of course, Tom continued to harass my nieces even after they moved out. He found out where they were living. They would find him sitting on the steps of their apartment waiting for them. As Amanda rounded the corner, she would spot him and run the other way. She would walk around the neighborhood for hours hoping he would not be there when she returned.

My niece's apartment was on the second floor and they could not see who was at the front door. One day Nicole opened the door because she thought it was FedEx with a package. To her shock, there stood Tom. He was in bad shape and insisted on coming in. He asked Nicole for vodka to ease his headache. He remained seated at her table drinking and complaining about Tommy. He said my nephew ate a lot of food and that Tom needed "me time" because he needed a break. Nicole snuck into the bedroom to call me. She was frantic. I told her to tell him to leave or call the police. She was terrified to do either. She did not want to trigger an outrage from him. He eventually left after five long grueling hours keeping her hostage.

Tom continued to harass Nicole for money. In reality, the social security money could have been enough to take care of the bills especially if he worked. He begged Nicole for money to repair the roof. He said it was leaking and would cost $4,000. Nicole gave him half the money. No repairs were done. It was just another scheme. She confronted Tom, and he then promised to pay her back $400 a week, which never happened. He told her that he also needed money to fix the floor in order to sell the house. Nicole wired the money into his friend Robin's bank account. I told her not to do it, but Nicole thought it was a legit reason and also wanted to keep Tom away and knew money would do so. Tom said Robin was a contractor who was going to fix the floor. Later we found out that Robin was Tom's new girlfriend.

Nicole called me panicking because Tom said that he needed $10,000 for Angela's hospital bill. I told Nicole to just try to remain calm and not to give him a penny! I will make sure that Angela's estate is legally settled and at that time any outstanding debt on my sister's behalf will be taken care of. The hospital bill will be paid if there is truly a balance. I told her that Tom was full of crap and to ask him for a copy of the hospital insurance statement. Nicole took a deep breath and called him back. She asked him for a copy of the hospital statement so that she could pay them directly. He told her not to worry that he took care of the hospital bill already. Nicole called me back with Tom's response. I replied, "Really? He paid the $10,000 hospital bill within the last five minutes?" We both understood that if Tom was backed into a corner, he would retreat.

When Tom disappeared the following month to party with the social security money, I told Nicole to call the local police precinct to file a missing person's report. We wanted the police to get involved and send someone to the house. This way, we could have proof and documentation that Tom left Tommy alone for an extended period of time. The police informed her that there was nothing they could do because it had only been twenty-four hours. They were focused on Tom's rights as an adult and not concerned about the safety of my nephew.

Tommy was scared of being left alone. The following morning, he took a taxi cab to Nicole's apartment to stay with her. That evening, there was still no sign of Tom. Tom's sister Donna then called the police. She explained that Tom had been missing for over thirty-six hours and left his son alone. The police officer said to her, "Well you said your nephew took a cab to his sister's house and that he is there now, so what's the problem?" It was obvious we were not going to get any assistance from the police department.

Nicole had been texting and calling her father throughout his two-day disappearance stunt. I was beginning to think that maybe something happened to him this time. I called the local hospitals to check if he was there. He had been missing for forty hours when Nicole finally received word from him. His story to her was that he was in jail because of the past due car registration. His story to Amanda was that he was in the emergency room. His story to Donna was that he was in the hospital because he got a bad throat infection from the jail. With all his crazy text messages, he never once asked where Tommy was or how Tommy was doing. Tom continued to stay missing for an additional two more days, making a total of four days that he abandoned his son.

CPS sent a representative to Nicole's apartment to question my nephew. She spoke with Tommy privately and he told her the truth. He told her that his father had left him alone overnight. The next morning, he took a cab to his sister's apartment and said that his dad would not answer his phone. We felt hopeful now that something could finally be done. After the report was filed, I received a phone call from the case worker. She told me that they had enough to proceed with a court hearing. They would start the process of removing Tommy from the house and grant me temporary custody. I could not believe my ears. I excitedly called Nicole and then the family lawyer. The lawyer went to the courthouse to represent me. I was elated that finally after eight months, Tommy was getting out of that dangerous situation.

I was on pins and needles waiting for the call from my lawyer, but when I heard what he said, I almost collapsed to the floor. He told me that I was not going to get custody because the court hearing was cancelled. He said it was a wasted trip to the court. I was hysterically crying. I immediately hung up the phone and called the case worker. She told me that they scheduled a meeting with Tom prior to the court hearing. During this meeting, my nephew retracted his story. My nephew said that his father was home and he was not left alone. Tommy said that Tom was in the basement the whole time.

The house is small and there was no way that Tom was hiding in the house for four days! She knew that my nephew was lying, but she had no choice but to cancel the court hearing. She was frustrated with both of them as well.

Sadly, the exact ordeal happened twice. Tom went missing for days. Tommy told the truth initially and then retracted his statement. Tommy confided in Nicole that Tom was intimidating and pressured him to lie. Our hopes were shattered. After the lawyer informed me of the second unsuccessful trip to court, this news pushed me to the tipping point of a complete nervous breakdown. He advised me to work on written testimony to present to the judge for our scheduled court date in August. I worked diligently documenting the neglect I knew of from the past year. My obsessive record-keeping came in handy. My nieces and husband also had to write their testimony for the court. Tom was served the court papers.

The following is Nicole's letter to the court:

> For a long as I know my father, people have been covering for him. He has always been unreliable, and we could never trust him or take his word on anything. Since I was twelve years old receiving an allowance from my mother or babysitting money from my aunts, I have always had to hide money from my father. It was understood that if my father found your money, he would take it and do what he wants with it. At twelve, I was hiding my money in a vitamin container in the bathroom cabinet, which he found and stole. This is just one example of what my father will do for money, steal from his twelve-year-old daughter, and of course this was not his worst offense.
>
> My mother had to pay to have our kitchen remodeled twice because my father was supposed to pay the contractor but instead took the money and used it on himself. It was a large amount

of money, over $10,000, which she had to pay again to the contractor. She could not even rely on him to go grocery shopping; she had to go with him. If she gave him money to get groceries when she got home from work, we were not getting the groceries and not seeing him again until the next day. So instead my mother had to do everything—work, cook, clean, and take care of all three of her children plus a husband with drug and money issues.

My parents always fought; at times it was violent. My mother would scream at him because he was out all night, and he would be hung over or possibly still high and would be very angry. I used to get scared because of his temper, and when their fighting woke me up at night or in the morning, I would lay awake in my bed and listen to make sure he did not hit her. They did not get violent very often, but he would threaten her, so it made me nervous.

My father is a sick man who has problems with drugs and alcohol. He used to drink a lot, but now he abuses cocaine more than anything else. I have never witnessed him taking cocaine, but my sister and I found dime bags under the couch and in the laundry. I know that my mother has tried to make him go to rehab in the past, but it never worked out. One reason I believe he is using cocaine is because he always has a runny nose and has had this "cold" for many years. On top of this, he has been hanging out with his brother who has admitted to family members that they both have been using cocaine, as well as a young girl named Erin who is known in my neighborhood to be a drug addict. Erin even made an appearance at my mother's funeral. At the funeral dinner, my father told Erin that he was going to receive my mother's life insurance money. I found this out through my other aunt and cousin who were seated with them. My father did not even pay for the funeral dinner. I did.

Since my mother had a stroke on June 23, I was taking care of all the bills, cooking, cleaning, laundry, grocery shopping and taking care of my younger brother Tommy. My sister Amanda would help me sometimes but my father never lifted a finger. He was never concerned with how we would pay the bills or have food to eat. Maybe he went grocery shopping a handful of times while my mother was in the hospital, but I am certain I could count those times on one hand. I was the power of attorney on my mother's account while she was in the hospital, and I handled all the finances. My mother knew she could not trust my father with anything. However, while she knew he was not trustworthy, she did not want anyone else to know that. Even while she was extremely sick over the summer, she would ask me if Tom's sister, my aunt, knew that I was her power of attorney and if I told her that. My mother wanted everyone to think our lives were perfect and that my father didn't have problems. No matter what he did, she made an excuse for him to others.

I cannot even count the amount of times my father has said he would be somewhere at a certain time and not show up or how many times he said he was going to "the store" at night and never come home, as well as countless times he needed to "borrow" money that he never paid back. We could never believe a word he said, because he is always only looking out for himself and his next fix.

While my mother was in the hospital, if and when my father showed up, he was high and would arrive late and not stay for long. He was never at home in the morning and did not have a job either. Maybe it was too hard for him to see his wife like that, but I still believe if he was not working, there was nowhere else he needed to be but by her side. My mother supported this man for twenty-six years and he was not there for her when she needed him the most.

I was working full time when my mother was in the hospital, but I took a leave of absence from my job because I needed to be with her. My mother could not speak or move and was in constant pain. She was in the hospital since June 23, and passed away on August 14, 2010, on a respirator the whole time suffering. During this time, my father went out very often and always asked me for money. My aunt Kate took my brother to her home in Virginia for a month so that it would be easier for me to be with my mother. I could not rely on my father to take care of my brother or the house or bills, and at that time, I did my best to do everything the way my mother did because I thought someday she may return home.

When my father was at the hospital and high, he was very belligerent and even got into an argument with his sister in front of my mother. Here this woman is dying but he has to go out every night, come to the hospital high, and get angry and yell in front of my mother to make her more upset. It was disgusting.

A few months after my mother passed away, I moved out. I could not handle living with my father any longer. In October, the inspection on our car expired, so I no longer had a car to go grocery shopping with. I would walk and make several trips to the store so I could carry all the groceries home. I did not get the car inspected because I was fed up that I had to do everything. To this day, the car still has not been inspected, showing how little my father will do. At one point, he was using his mother's car, which is in horrendous condition. My father's mother has Alzheimer's and is therefore extremely forgetful. He told her that someone broke into her car and it was in no condition to be driven. He told her this so she would not try to drive it, but instead he took the car and was using it. He also stole money from his mother's bank account. He would take her to the bank for withdrawals once her social security money came in. He would tell his mother she must have misplaced it and she would believe him. My mother's car and grand-mother's car went "missing" while under my father's use.

My father will steal from anyone. He has stolen money from me, my bike, and even Halloween decorations. He doesn't care how anyone feels as long as it benefits him. He will do anything to get money out of someone, and that's why he wants to keep my brother here living with him. In October, my brother Tommy told me he wanted to move to my aunt Kate's house in Virginia. My father agreed to it but mentioned to Tommy that it would mess him up with receiving the social security money. That is all he cares about. Like I said, he is a sick man. He got Tommy to stay living with him by buying my brother a gaming system. If there was no money attached to my brother, my father would have no interest in keeping him in New York.

My father does not take him to the doctor or for counseling, which he so desperately needs. My brother's glasses leave marks on his face because they are so old and rusting, and he needs a new prescription. I have brought this up to my father several times, and he still has not taken him. He says he will but he will always tell you what you want to hear. My brother has not had a haircut in over a year. Tommy also told me there is often not a lot of food in the house. Of course, my father blames the lack of food on Tommy because he says Tommy eats too much. My father often says negative things about Tommy, and my father has said to me that he spends too much time with him and he "needs a break from him."

Tommy would be much better off living with Aunt Kate and Uncle Paul in Virginia. They have a peaceful, structured home and family. They are very involved in their children's lives and spend a lot of quality time with them. They often have family outings, and someone is always home with the children. The house is always clean, and there is healthy food on the table. Aunt Kate's children are never made to feel as though they are a burden, eat too much, or are unwanted. This is how my father makes Tommy feel as he has told me he doesn't think my dad cares about him. If he spends "quality" time with Tommy, it is at a bar, not a park or church.

My aunt Kate has twin boys that are fourteen and my brother Tommy is thirteen. They are very close and I think they would be great for Tommy to be around. He does not interact with children of his age now because he is just living with my father and is on the computer playing games most of the time. I know Kate would love and take care of my brother as if he were her own. I know that she would take him to the doctor, to church and get him counseling.

There was a time a few years ago when my brother had to go to the emergency room when he was bleeding from his nose and eyes. My mother was already at work and I do not remember where my father was. I was very scared and was supposed to leave for work, but I did not know what to do, so I called my aunt Kate. She came to get me and my brother right away and took us to the hospital where she stayed with my brother. She loves us very much and would do anything for us. We have always been close.

I tried to say as much as I could about my father at our Child Protective Services meetings, but he gets very defensive and tries to get Tommy to lie for him. My father is also very intimidating, and it is hard to get everything out in front of him. He asked me to lie for him prior to the meetings and started yelling at my sister, my aunt Donna and me as soon as we walked into the Child Protective Services building.

He has left my brother alone several nights at a time since I moved out. The last time was the worst. He was missing for four days and did not even know where his son was. My brother has told me at night he is alone till 4:00 a.m. or possibly all night. I always offer to get him a cab to come over because I do not want him to be alone.

When my father surfaced after being gone for four days, he texted my brother asking him where he was, showing that my father did not know where Tommy had gone. Another time

I had my brother stay at my apartment for a weekend and my aunt Donna was going to drive Tommy back home Sunday night. We drove by my father's house and he was not home, so we called him and he cursed at me and got very angry that my aunt Donna now knew that he was not home. He told Donna at 9:00 p.m. that he would be home in thirty minutes. Donna drove Tommy back to my apartment, and we waited to hear from my father, which he never did. He sent me a text at five thirty the next morning asking if Tommy was still with me or if he was at my uncle James's house. Again my father had no idea where his son was. He eventually picked Tommy up from my apartment at seven thirty that morning. These are only two examples but he had left Tommy alone often, and it is usually in the middle of the month when my father receives the social security checks.

I am very worried about my brother's future. If he continues to live with my father, he will continue to be neglected and quite possibly will go down the wrong path. I know Aunt Kate would take care of everything that Tommy needs. She sincerely wants him and loves him. With my father, it is all about the money. I would love my father to let Tommy go to Virginia and for him to go to rehab and get help. I want my father to rebuild his life, but at this point, Tommy's well-being is what is most important.

The decision was still in Tom's hands as the court date was approaching. Tom did not want the responsibility of his child and I hoped in his heart he wanted Tommy cared for. In an effort to avoid the stress of going to court, I decided to send a final letter as a last effort.

Tom,

I know losing Angela has taken its toll on all of us. She was such a special caring person and you know how close we were. She confided in me over the years, and I know about your addictions and infidelities. We are not as clueless as you think. I begged her over the years to either force you to get help or get a divorce. It sickens me to know about all the stuff she and your children endure because of your actions.

Even through it all, Angela still loved you. I guess Angela felt the best way to handle things was to cover for you, which only enabled you more. Your children were conditioned to do the same. I don't know if you even realize all the emotional and physical scarring your behavior has caused to your family. Angela was always sick with her headaches because she kept all the stress bottled up, and it ultimately took her life. You are a sick man and addiction is a serious disease. You have chosen your lifestyle endless times over the welfare of your family. I know you feel everyone is against you, but you are in such deep denial. Your family would graciously support you if you were sincere about getting help. You have the ability and free will to change your future.

You wallow in self-pity and feel like you are always the victim. The real victims are your children. It had to be a nightmare what Angela put up with, but she also contributed to the situation by allowing it. Your children are the innocent ones who have suffered living in a household filled with conflict and pain. Do you feel any sympathy or compassion for anyone else who is suffering because of the loss of Angela like your children and her family members and friends? You are not the only one suffering.

We cannot even grieve Angela properly because of all the added stress you caused. You have never been held accountable for any of your actions. But you had the free will to make your own decisions. You need to take a deep look into yourself. One day you will have to answer to a higher power. I know you are a tormented soul and you are in pain. I am not heartless but my concern is first for the welfare and safety of Tommy. I would be overjoyed if you ever got the help you need. You are the only one who can change your life and you need to admit you have an addiction. It is all up to you. No one can fix you. That was Angela's mistake. You are the only one who can fix yourself. But I am telling you everyone would admire you and support you if you did.

I am offering to take Tommy and provide a loving, caring, nurturing safe home. This is what Angela wanted. I am trying to honor her dying wish. You need to be a responsible parent and consider what is best for your son and daughters. The stress is emotionally and physically taking its toll on all of your children. You have let the demons of addiction control you. Your actions during their young lives have scarred them deeply. You need to consider what is best for Tommy's future. He is at a very impressionable age. You can make the right choice now and let Tommy stay with me. I want you to continue to be in Tommy's life, and I also want you to get the help you desperately need. You can then start to rebuild your life and your relationships with your children and family. The choice is yours.

You cannot leave the decision to a traumatized twelve-year-old child who has received no counseling for the tremendous loss of his mother.

We can still work this out. Please call me and let me know what you want to do. We can avoid going to court. I know drugs and alcohol abuse changes people but look deep in your heart and do the right thing. God has blessed you with three wonderful children and a family who will support you 100 percent if you choose to get help. You can rebuild your life and career. If not, people will distance themselves from you because a relationship with you right now is toxic and unhealthy. It is time to let some healing begin, and you can control this by doing what is right for yourself and your family. Do it for the love of Angela and for the love of your children. Tommy's future lies in your hands.

I am enclosing Angela's eulogy for you to read. Do you want to be remembered for all the pain and suffering you caused? Do you want to be remembered as a father who was stricken with an illness but had the courage to change?

Sincerely,
Kate

Tom did not reply to my letter. However, he did allow Tommy to stay with me once the school year ended. Tommy lived with us for several months before the court date. I thought this was crazy on Tom's part, but I was glad to have my nephew here. This would allow my nephew to experience what his life could be like living with us. I immediately made all the necessary arrangements for Tommy to fly to Virginia before Tom changed his mind.

When Tommy arrived at our house, I was overtaken by his physical appearance and horrendous odor. It was apparent that he had not been bathing properly. His greasy matted long hair hung covering his entire face. I made him wash his hair, but the grease would not come out. I asked him if I could wash his hair for him. I explained that he needed a deep clean, which he allowed. I had to be very gentle because there were scabs covering his scalp.

I washed all of his stained clothes several times to get rid of the cigarette and cat urine odor on them. Tommy was not taking care of his hygiene and neither was his father. What emotional state was this poor child in? It broke my heart seeing this neglect, and I knew he must have been picked on at school.

I attempted to speak to Tommy about his father and explain the court process. He refused to talk about it and said he was never going to live in Virginia. Tommy was still in denial and not processing. All I could do was provide love and care to him and wait for the court date. Our court date was set for August 17, which was the date that we buried my sister the year prior.

CHAPTER 19

Several weeks later, the priest's homily focused on how keeping anger in your heart was a sin. This triggered me to receive the Sacrament of Reconciliation. During my confession, I briefly explained to the priest about the past year and my harbored anger toward my brother-in-law. He told me that God trusted me with the children and to take comfort in that. Tom would have to live with his choices and that I should just focus on how much God believes in me. The Holy Spirit then led me to a lecture on forgiveness given by a priest named Father William Meninger. I read his book, *The Process of Forgiveness*, before attending the lecture.

I learned forgiveness is not necessarily about the person who wronged you, but is about freedom. Most of the time, the person who has wronged you will not ask for forgiveness. You will always be disappointed waiting for them to ask for forgiveness. During his lecture, Father Meninger stated you have to learn to forgive even if the person never apologizes; otherwise you will be trapped in your hurt. Forgiveness will set you free. I struggled with that concept until he said forgiveness does not mean forgetting or excusing the wrong that had occurred. Forgiveness is not a form of absolution. People will have to answer for what they have done. This is up to them, not you. Only God gives absolution.

I had thought that my past hurts were healed but were reopened during this difficult time in my life as they resurfaced with a vengeance. People always say, "Time heals all wounds," but I felt time festered wounds instead. I took notes on Father Meninger's words of wisdom. He said that prayer gives us access to God's love. We need to forgive ourselves as well in order to free us from our self-imposed prisons. When we allow ourselves to remain wounded, our bitter resentment contaminates not only ourselves but also everyone we come into contact with. We then set ourselves up for repeated patterns of abuse, violence and rejection.

Memories of past suffering will always be there, but they do not have to be as painful. Forgiveness gives us power and freedom. It releases us from being stuck in the cruel events of our past, which may have stopped the progress of our lives. Forgiveness builds our self-esteem allowing us to know that we are more than victims because we had the courage and strength to forgive. Forgiveness is a slow gradual process in which healing is the result. Most wounds are inflicted by people who are closest to us. These wounds are the most painful, lasting and traumatic and they allow the child we were to still live on within us.

Father Meninger's lecture outlined the stages of forgiveness. The following are the notes that I took.

- Stage 1: Denial. Examine the hurt and claim it. Do not try to minimize or deny it. Our wounds are part of us. We must accept them and the scars that have resulted.
- Stage 2: Guilt. Reluctant to put blame entirely on the wrongdoer because it may be someone close to you. Must be my fault as well.
- Stage 3: Victim. This should only be a stage, not a permanent lifestyle. It gives us a way to finally get the sympathy attention we should have received when we were first wounded.
- Stage 4: Anger. Positive anger is normal and should be expressed, not suppressed. Repressed anger manifests with anxiety and takes a physical toll.
- Final state: Wholeness[7]

---

[7]   William Meninger, O.C.S.O., *The Process of Forgiveness* (NY, Bloomsbury, 1996), pp. 48–72.

It was insightful to learn about the stages and to realize which stage I was in. Final healing leaves a scar, but the injured tissue is stronger than it was before the wound was inflicted. Forgiveness is a choice. We do not even have to tell the offender that we forgive. In fact, the person we need to forgive may be deceased. We do not need to restore relationships with the person who has wronged us.

Self-forgiveness is to understand that no one is perfect. It is essential to stop punishing yourself for past mistakes and sins that you are truly sorry for. God can forgive us and we can forgive ourselves. We hold onto the guilt that keeps us in chains. Forgiveness is the way to unlock the chains to grow and heal.

Father Meninger introduced us to Compassion Meditation Prayer as a method of forgiveness which is outlined below.

- Close your eyes as you pray.
- Recall as vividly and realistically as you can someone (living or deceased) who loves you and who you love and recapture and even intensify your feeling of love for that person. Pray the Compassion Meditation Prayer for him or her.
- Choose an indifferent person, a stranger, or a mere acquaintance. Give to this indifferent person the feeling and the quality of love you have for the loved person above. Pray the Compassion Meditation Prayer for him or her.
- Choose an enemy (living or deceased) and transfer the energy of the love you have for your loved one and the indifferent person. Pray the Compassion Meditation Prayer for him or her.

Compassion Meditation Prayer

May you be happy. May you be free.
May you be loving. May you be loved.
May you come to the perfect fulfillment of what
    God has planned for you.
May you recognize yourself as a beloved son or
    daughter of God.

May you receive and grow in the fullness of the
graces Jesus has won for you.
May you receive grace, peace and fellowship in
the Father, Son and Holy Spirit.
May you know true peace.
May all good things be yours.
May every fiber of your being resonate to the
glory to which God calls you.
May you know the Lord in all his goodness and
compassion.
May you be forgiven every transgression.
I forgive you your every transgression with all my
heart.
May Almighty God bless you and keep you, show
his countenance to you, and give you peace.[8]

He told us to practice this prayer in order to forgive those who
have wronged us. My question was, "How do you know when you
are fully healed?" His response was, "When your hurt or the one who
has wronged you no longer has a hold on you."

I was grateful for the gift that God led me to this retreat. I knew
it would provide the groundwork to accept whatever the custody
outcome would be even though I was still distraught at the thought
of not gaining custody of my nephew. During the Sunday Mass prior
to the court date, the words "Thy Will" really stayed with me. The
words were crystal clear just like the words I heard in the shower,
"Save the children." It was truly God's will and not my will as to the
outcome from the court. I had no control of the situation anymore. I
felt a peaceful resolve realizing that I did not fail my sister but indeed
kept my promise to her. I had done everything humanly possible
over the past year to try to get custody of her son. Now it was in
God's hands only.

---

8 Meninger, p.121–125.

CHAPTER 20

I knew Nicole was struggling with her mixed feelings toward her father. She loved her father because he was her father. But at the same time, she felt disgust toward him. She understood that their relationship was dysfunctional, and she wanted to be free from him. I reminded Nicole what the oncologist said, "The only way to cure cancer is to cut it out." I told her that a relationship with her father right now was like a cancer and he was poison. If he was sincere about getting the help he needed, then that would be different. She wanted to reach out to speak to him but was afraid. I made the suggestion to write him a letter. This would allow her to collect her thoughts and not regret her words.

Nicole sent this letter to her father.

> You were right. I did turn my phone off. It is something you have done many times before. When you were gone for four days, you had your phone off and didn't have to answer to anyone about where you were. When Mom was going into cardiac arrest one night at the hospital, you were out with Erin when the hospital tried to call you. I was the only one home comforting Amanda when she was having a meltdown since the hospital couldn't reach you. They called her and said, "Hurry! Your mother may not make it."

You don't care how hurt she was. You have not asked any of us once since our mother got sick how we feel. It is all about you.

I know Aunt Kate filing for custody may not work, but at least she has to try. You keep stressing that you were home last Wednesday and Thursday and that is the truth and I should believe you. Why should I? You never tell the truth and you always twist the story. To say you never talk about money to Tommy is a lie. Money is *all* that you talk about.

At Mom's funeral dinner, you were bragging to Erin and your friends that you were getting her insurance money, and you think that is normal behavior? When you were at my house a few Sundays ago, you were ranting and raving about money all day as well as threatening everyone in the family. Why should I have to be exposed to this? Clearly the system works in your favor and supports you. At the last Child Protective Services meeting, they said I have to let go of some of my resentment. Why do I have to when you don't care how you have hurt me and you think you have never done anything wrong? I have all the right in the world to be hurt and angry.

Do not call or text me to threaten Aunt Donna anymore. She came to the meetings to support me because I needed her. It has nothing to do with you. She does it for me. She is an amazing woman and would even support you if you asked for help and would forgive you if you apologized to her. You have said such hurtful things about her children when they have done nothing to you. Nobody would ever attack your children or say anything negative about us to you because it is not right. You get angry at her because she has confronted you in the past when the rest of your family is too scared to do so. I am sure you talk badly about me and curse me out to Tommy and others too. I know you do. But you don't curse me out when you need money or you are eating and drinking at my apartment.

You don't care about how I feel or what I think. Where are my Halloween decorations or my bike? You steal and take whatever you want without asking and think we should just forgive you when you have never once asked for forgiveness. You just take and take. You said to Amanda she was the only one who said happy Father's Day to you. Why should I say happy Father's Day? Did you even acknowledge my last birthday? No. You didn't wish me a happy birthday or even get me a card or cake. Do you know what you did instead? You asked me for $100. On Amanda's birthday, you were missing as usual and did not say happy birthday to her either. We had to look all over for someone to watch Tommy.

You are always short on money and come to me. The only time I hear from you is when you want money or when you want to bring Tommy over for me to watch. How dare you say at the Child Protective Service meetings that I never spend time with my brother! I see him almost every weekend because you do not want to take care of him. You tell them at the meetings that you need "me time." I work full time and then I have to take care of Tommy on the weekends while you haven't worked a steady job in years. You have all the "me time" in the world. How can you say you don't care about the social security money? You admitted back in October that if Tommy went to Virginia, it would screw you up, not because you would not have your son around, but because of the social security money. Those were your *exact* words.

If Tommy wants to stay with you, fine. That is his decision. But he cannot play both sides like he has been. He wants to live with you during the week and live with me on the weekends. He can't control the situation either. What he tells you and what he tells me are completely different stories. If he wants to lie and cover for you, that is his choice. He is old enough to realize what is going on and he can make his own decisions. I had at least tried to do the right thing for Tommy because I care about his future. You have chosen your lifestyle over us many times, and I have lived through that. I know what lies ahead for Tommy and it concerns me. That is why I speak up at the Child Protective Services meetings, not because I was trying to get you in trouble or attack you. I did it for my brother.

I spent almost every minute of every day with my mother in the hospital, and she told me a lot of things. My mother knew she was dying and told Aunt Kate to take care of Tommy. She knew that is where he would be best taken care of, nurtured and loved. The only last wish of hers that you want me to honor is paying your mortgage and you say you don't care about money. I know it is a chore for you to have Tommy, just by the way you speak to him in front of me, it is very disturbing. You said that Tommy eats too much food and gets on your nerves. I'm sure you think what you say is not disturbing, so we will have to agree to disagree on that.

Stop harassing me like you have been. Don't call me to yell at me about this letter. You don't get to be in control and dictate my life anymore. If you want to e-mail me, you can. I don't want to speak. I only want to hear from you if it has to do with Tommy coming over or arrangements that have to do with him. I don't need the stress of dealing with you in my life. It has already made me sick as I have an ulcer and throw up every day from this stress. I don't need it and I won't deal with it any longer. If you want to go for counseling and get help and get counseling for my brother, we can talk. I won't step into Mom's shoes and support you or cover for you. You can take care of yourself. This is not a healthy father-daughter relationship. This is torture.

Nicole

This letter represented the start of Nicole's independence from Tom's grip. He never replied to the letter.

CHAPTER 21

After the longest year of my life, the court date was finally approaching. I flew back to New York with my nephew and dropped him off with his father. The hearing was set for the following morning, and I prayed that Tom would show up. I met my nieces outside of the courthouse. I was so happy to see them. We were extremely anxious as we entered the courthouse. This was the first time I met the lawyer face-to-face after months of phone calls. He directed us to the waiting room where we sat for several hours. Tom and Tommy arrived late but did show up. It was very awkward while we sat on the wooden bench in one row with Tom seated across from us. No one spoke.

My lawyer would come out from behind the closed doors to give me updates. He said the judge requested to assign an attorney to represent my nephew. My nephew's lawyer spoke to him in private to ask who he wanted to live with. My lawyer explained that this hearing was held by a mediation judge who has reviewed all the written testimony. If both parties could reach an agreement during this hearing, then it would be finished. If not, a preliminary court case would have to be set for a future date in which my nieces and nephew would need to testify in court. I was taken aback because I had no idea. I thought that today was the actual court hearing. The news sickened me to think this process could continue to drag on.

All the lawyers then proceeded back into the room without us. Ten minutes later, my lawyer approached me. He informed me that the judge would like to offer me temporary custody. I jumped at the offer, but after a few minutes of thinking about it, I pulled my lawyer aside. I told him, "I cannot take temporary custody. I know what will happen. I will take Tommy back to live with me, but as soon as Tom runs out of money, he will want to take Tommy back." I told the lawyer that we would have to proceed with another court date. I was emotionally deflated. This ordeal was not over, but now starting with a new beginning. My lawyer nodded and went back into the hearing.

To my surprise, he returned a few minutes later. He asked if I would agree to partial custody in which Tommy lives with me in Virginia. He said that this way, Tom doesn't feel like he gave Tommy up. I would be Tommy's legal guardian and we would not have to proceed with a full court hearing. The lawyers, Tom and I went into the hearing in front of the judge. Tom said that he planned on moving to Virginia to be closer to his son. This news threw me into a new panic. My lawyer whispered to me, "He most likely will never move and maybe visit Tommy once or twice a year." The judge ruled for joint custody in which my nephew would reside with me. The judge also added that I could work out visitation arrangements suitable for me. My lawyer said I could petition for child support from Tom but I declined. I did not want to upset the ruling. We signed the necessary papers and it was done. I could not believe it. I hugged and thanked my lawyer. He turned to me and said, "You are a good aunt."

I ran over to my nieces and told them the outcome. Tom approached us and asked if we wanted to get some lunch. I was sick to my stomach and food was the last thing on my mind. I thought, *This man is truly demented to think we want to have lunch with him.* We came up with some excuse. Tommy went back to the house with Tom to start packing. We headed back to the girl's apartment because they wanted to get some sleep. I called my mother, brother and husband sharing the bittersweet news. They were all excited but oddly I felt very sad. I tried to get some rest but could not sleep. I laid there crying instead. That evening, we decided to head over to the house. I wanted to make sure Tommy's stuff was packed even though he said he did on the phone.

I had to force myself to enter the house again and discovered that my sister's meticulously clean house was now a complete mess. The house was destroyed and in ruins. None of Tommy's things were packed. We started packing up as much as we could. It was a struggle working with my nephew to figure out what he wanted to take. We ended up ordering food and shared a meal with Tom. The next day, my friend drove us to the airport. It was heartbreaking taking my nephew from his home as we left Tom standing at the doorway.

My nephew had many emotional and physical issues to address once he moved in. I had to be delicate and sensitive with him. The first thing I dealt with was his hygiene and counseling. Tommy would not make eye contact with me as he tried to explain his difficulties in school. He was not doing his homework. I had to encourage him to complete the sentence he was struggling with when he was trying to explain his schoolwork. I could see the difficulties he was having just forming his thoughts. We came up with a plan for him to write down his assignments daily, which I reviewed. I had the ability to check his school status online and spoke with all his teachers. I noticed that he never did his class work and was getting a zero on the assignment. It took several months before my nephew was diagnosed with Attention-Deficit Hyperactivity Disorder (ADHD), Inattentive Type. This type of ADHD is easier to detect in the middle school years when a child is held accountable for his work and assignments. Tommy started taking medicine after his evaluation. His grades rocketed and all of his work was completed on time. His teacher told me that he was the most improved student she has ever had. He was starting to come out of his shell and making his own friends as well.

My emotional reality felt like I had experienced a divorce from Tom. Putting my feelings aside, I did not want to bad-mouth Tommy's father. I also wanted to explain to Tommy why we fought so hard to have him live with us. It continued to be a challenge to reach my nephew. I told him that his relationship with his father is different than the relationship his father has with his sisters.

Tom never called me to check on his son. I am sure if he had, our relationship would have been a little different. In the beginning, I used to sneak a look at my nephew's phone messages to see if Tom texted him. There were a few messages between the two of them but their correspondence was juvenile in nature. Tommy continued to defend his father, which hurt me over the years. I made a decision to stop reading the messages because I was just hurting myself. Tommy may never truly understand his father's past behavior and I had to accept that. I also knew that in Tommy's heart, he felt the love we had for him and why we fought so hard for his well-being. Shortly, after he moved in with us, he asked Nicole to take him shopping. He told her that he wanted to buy me a birthday present. At the store he picked out a necklace. The necklace will always be special to me but the real gift was his thoughtful gesture.

CHAPTER 22

My sister's children all experienced emotional trauma and needed guidance, support and love. Slowly relationships began to realign into their proper perspective. I had to encourage other family members as well not to look at Nicole as Tommy's second mother. It was disturbing to hear Amanda state that this was the first time in her life that she felt like herself. But it also meant that things were headed in the right direction.

Tom continued living in New York at the house until it was on the brink of foreclosure. He never paid the mortgage that year. Tom attempted to sell the house illegally because his name was not on the deed. His lawyer would send us letters to sign and requested copies of our passport, which I thought was bizarre. I called the estate lawyer whom I spoke with the year prior. He took our case and worked with Nicole. Nicole obtained a reputable realtor in order to sell the house. Thankfully the lawyer represented Nicole at the closing. She did not need to physically be there and was able to avoid seeing her father. The sale of the house along with my sister's estate was properly settled.

At the closing, our lawyer informed me that Tom stated Nicole ran up $2,000 in parking tickets and she needed to be the one responsible for paying them. I told the lawyer that was not true because she did not drive the car due to the expired registration. I told the lawyer to ask Tom where my sister's car was. I informed him that the car went missing as well as his mother's car and that

Tom is the Bermuda triangle of cars. Angela's car was her property, which should be part of her estate. The lawyer questioned Tom about the car. Tom did not have an answer and told the lawyer that he would pay for the parking tickets. The lawyer agreed that Tom was bad news after he dealt with Tom's temper at the closing. Tom received a large sum of money from the sale of the house. He still did not move to Virginia. He moved in with his new girlfriend in her mother's house in Staten Island.

Tommy invited his father to his middle school graduation. If Tom decided to come to the graduation, this would have been the first time Tommy saw his father since the move. I received a text message from Tom asking if he could stay the night at my house. Again I had to wonder, *"How delusional is this man?"* His son had been living with me for over a year and this is the first time I heard from him. I texted Tom back making it crystal clear that I will do my best raising his son, but he is never welcome in my house. I had to be blunt to get through to him. My nieces decided not to attend the graduation because they could not deal with seeing their father. I sat at the graduation feeling uptight as I kept scanning the audience looking for Tom. He arrived in the doorway late and missed Tommy's graduation. The plan was for Tommy to go back with Tom for a visit. I got the address and had no choice but to let him go. I was a nervous wreck and sick to my stomach.

Several years later, my nephew underwent major thoracic surgery. It was painful to see Tommy wheeled into the recovery room. I fought back my tears and the flashbacks of my sister. When my nieces came to visit their brother, they broke into tears because he resembled my sister so much. I slept overnight at the hospital and took my vacation time to spend the week at the hospital with Tommy. During that week, there were no texts, calls or visits from his father. After that, I was done. Tommy could keep a relationship with his father, but I was not going to get involved with their plans. I decided Tom was not worth my time and attention anymore.

Tommy continued to visit his father a few times a year. Eventually, Tom ended up in trouble in Staten Island. I kept getting harassing phone calls from collection agencies and investigators looking for Tom. I knew he was in trouble regarding another missing car. His trouble led him to move out of Staten Island and move right into my neighborhood. Of course, I was fearful about this move.

CHAPTER 23

I tried to focus on the positive things in my life and give less attention to the negative things. At the same time, I noticed my spiritual life started to have an inner voice. When thoughts and ideas lingered with me, I felt a spiritual energy to write them down. What started out as an ordinary day became an extraordinary day to me. The event took place with me, my sons Ethan and Ryan and my nephew Tommy. The experience motivated me to create the following piece, *The Wise Men*.

The Wise Men

My story of the three wise men began on a family trip to the guitar store. While we were all browsing around the store for several hours, an individual came into the guitar store. He sat down on the chair Ethan was previously sitting on trying out new guitars. This man was of average height. He had wild brown hair accompanied with a full face of hair. He wore battered old clothes and emitted an offensive body odor.

After we made our purchase, we decided to go for lunch and asked if we could come back for our merchandise. During lunch, I kept thinking of this homeless man and I announced that I wanted to bring him my leftover food. My announcement sparked a conversation with all three boys because they did not realize he was homeless. So we all returned to the car and headed back to the guitar store. At this time, Ethan was concerned that the man would have left and asked, "What if he is gone? What will we do then?" We arrived at the store and Ethan was excited when he spotted the man. He was sitting outside the store on the ground with his back against a pillar.

The twins and I got out of the car to bring him my lunch and to retrieve the guitars. As I walked over to him, I thought, "How will this man respond to me?" I pushed the negative thoughts out of my head and stood next to him. He was sitting there with his head bent forward. As I addressed him, he slowly raised his head, turned, and looked up at me. I cannot explain the feeling I felt as I looked into the most amazing crystal clear blue eyes. I can't even describe the color, for it was a shade of blue I have never seen before. All I knew was that I was looking into the eyes of no ordinary man. It took my breath away, and then I found my voice to ask him if he would like some food.

He responded in a soft spoken voice, "Yes, thank you." I asked if he would like more, so I hurried back to the car. I asked my nephew Tommy if he would give up his leftover food and he generously agreed. I turned to Ryan and told him to bring the food to the man. Ryan approached him, and my heart swelled with pride when I heard Ryan said, "Excuse me, sir."

That day, this stranger received the gifts from three wise men—concern, generosity and respect. I too received a gift of being part of this exchange and the privilege of looking into those eyes. But if you think about it, if you really look deep into someone's eyes, you too will see God, for God is in all of us.

Kate Lynn Winters

CHAPTER 24

We celebrated the twin's high school graduation along with my niece Amanda's college graduation with a circus-themed party. Throughout the years, all the milestones especially regarding my sister's children were bittersweet without her. I know my sister was with us in spirit, but it still pained me that she was not physically there. As Nicole and I were inside setting up for the party with our amazing decorations, Amanda ran into the clubhouse out of breath. She hurriedly told us to come outside. We dropped what we were doing and quickly ran outside. All three of us stood in awe facing forward holding hands.

I turned to my nieces and said, "This is definitely from your mother to show you how very proud she is of each of you and that she loves us all so very much." We could not take our eyes off the most vibrant, full, biggest rainbow arching across the sky right in front of us.

Years later, I was awakened from a nightmare. In my dream, I was planning on renovating my childhood house in order to move back in. As I descended into the basement, the floor and walls were covered with crawling bugs, and I was immediately grossed out. I questioned my friend, "How am I supposed to live here in this house?" I pointed out to her all the water damage and rotten, decaying wooden beams that were supposed to support the house. We walked through the basement door to enter the garage. As we opened the door, a huge rat ran out in front of us. I screamed as the rat ran down into a deep hole. I quickly grabbed a metal plate to cover the hole. The rat kept jumping and was trying to push the plate up. My friend told me that there must be a nest of rats. I panicked and hurried into the garage searching for concrete cinder blocks. I stacked them on top of the plate cover to keep the rats trapped inside. I said I was calling the exterminator. In my dream, I felt upset about killing the rats, but I knew I had to get rid of these pests in order to live in the house.

The next evening, I had another nightmare. There was a lake where this enormous crocodile was hiding. Every once in a while, he would surface as his dark menacing eyes stared straight at me. I was standing at the water's edge, and I desperately needed to reach this small house across the lake. I knew my family was in the house, but I was too terrified to get into the water. As I attempted to step one foot into the lake to swim across, the crocodile would arise and slowly turn his head in my direction. I quickly took my foot out of the water to step back onto the land. I made a second attempt and immersed myself into the lake. The dream frightened me awake. I kept thinking of those strange dreams, so I decided to look into the interpretation of them.

Dreams of bugs symbolize fears and anxieties. Bugs in dreams may also indicate being bullied by someone. They also signify someone in your life who you do not like or someone who disgusts you.

A dream of a rat represents a person that cannot be trusted, an enemy or someone who is capable of deception. A rat in a dream could be a symbol of things you wish to forget in your life.

A dream of a rotting house or decay is usually a warning and symbolizes obstacles.

Dreams of crocodiles symbolize freedom and hidden strength. Crocodile dreams are a forewarning about an impending danger lurking around you. Things are becoming clearer in your life and you are about to become more aware of your surroundings.

My dream interpretations led me to the conclusion of my freedom from the bugs, rats and the danger of the crocodile in my life. I was able to rebuild a safe sound house for my family to dwell in.

CHAPTER 25

There was a course offered at our church called Living Your Strengths. The purpose of this course was to discover the talents God has given us from birth and to take steps toward recognizing them. If we listen to God's guidance, our talents could be developed into our strengths. We can then use our strengths for the benefit of our community in order to serve others. It is also essential to recognize and be attuned to other's talents.

The course began with a twenty-minute online test that requires quick and honest answers to various situations presented in the questions. The test formulated my top five talents. Everyone has their own unique top five talents. It is very rare to have the same talents and in the same order as anyone else. The next few weeks were spent examining each talent. Learning about my talents made me realize why I respond in certain ways to certain situations that arise in my life.

My top five talents were responsibility, belief, connectedness, arranger and developer.

- Responsibility. The responsibility theme forces you to take psychological ownership for anything you commit to, whether large or small. You feel emotionally bound to follow through to completion. The obsession for doing things right combined with impeccable ethics creates your reputation, which is utterly dependable.

- Belief. Belief theme causes you to be family-oriented, to be spiritual, and to value responsibility. You have high ethics both in yourself and in others. The core values affect your behavior in many ways. These values give your life meaning and satisfaction. Your view of success is more than money and prestige, but it is the foundation of all your relationships. Your friends call you dependable and your beliefs make you easy to trust. Your work must be meaningful to you and needs to matter.

- Connectedness. With the connectedness theme, you believe things happen for a reason and you are sure of it. In your soul, you know that we are all connected. You understand individuals are responsible for our own judgment and possess their own free will, but nonetheless we are part of something larger. Your faith is strong as it sustains you in the face of life's mysteries. Connectedness talents are valuable providing you with conviction and faith that sustains and encourages you in difficult times. Connectedness gives you hope and helps you to achieve your ultimate goals.

- Developer. In your view, no individual is fully formed and is a constant work in progress. You see potential in others as they are alive with possibilities. You devise interesting experiences that can stretch them and help them grow to experience success. Their signs of growth are what fuels you because your helpfulness is genuine and sincere. Applying your developer talent, you are educating, counseling and encouraging people all the time.

- Arranger. You are a highly organized conductor. When faced with complex situations, you enjoy managing all the variables. You align and realign them until you are sure you have arranged them in the most productive configuration possible. Because after all, you know there just might be a better way. You simply try to figure out the best way to get things done. Those lacking this theme may ask, "How can you keep so many things in your head at once?"[9]

It was incredible how my top five talents truly described me to a tee. It was no wonder why I felt so compelled to keep my promise to my sister. It also explained why I was so outraged over the past year. The course pointed out that my talents need to be kept in balance because overdoing one talent may lead to negative results.

Each of us has a calling and we just need to discover what it is. We all have our own unique God-given spiritual gifts, talents and strengths that make up our composition. God has a role for each of us to play in his plan. The calling doesn't come from God's voice thundering from above but may come from his soft whispers deep within us. As we discover our talents, then we can begin to discover our calling. As we build our strengths by making the most of our talents, then we can fulfill our calling.

I believed God called me to "Save the children" because he knew how he made me. Responsibility was my top talent, which propelled me into action. With belief and connectedness, God knew that I would never give up the fight throughout the year to help my family. The arranger and developer talents were put into good use dealing with the struggles presented with my nephew's ongoing issues. Those talents assisted me in guiding and helping him overcome obstacles one at a time as he grew into an outstanding young man.

One of the leaders read the following words that she felt summed up the contents of the class.

> Our deepest fear is not that we are inadequate.
> Our deepest fear is that we are powerful beyond
> measure.
> It is our light, not our darkness, that frightens us
> most.

---

[9]   Donald O. Clifton, PH. D, Curt Liesveld, M.Div., M.A., Albert Weisman, D. Min., *Living Your Strengths* (NY, Gallup Press, 2006), pp.63–148.

We ask ourselves, Who am I to be brilliant, gor-
geous, talented and fabulous?
Actually, who are you not to be?
You are a child of God. Your playing small doesn't
serve the world.
There is nothing enlightened about shrinking so
that other people won't feel insecure around
you.
We were born to make manifest the glory of God
within us.
It is not just in some of us. It's in everyone.
And as we let our light shine, we unconsciously
give other people permission to do the same.
As we are liberated from our own fear, our presence automatically liberates others.[10]

I continued learning by attending another course on charisms.
Charisms are supernatural gifts given to us from the Holy Spirit. It
allows God to work through us so that these gifts are received by
others. The intention is to help others. We are only the vessel in
which God works through if we are willing to accept the calling.
Even though charisms are not for our own purpose, we may receive
the awesome experience of love by witnessing the happiness, peace
and joy one may receive. The focus of the class was to assist us in
discerning which charism we may have. I took another test that suggested the possible charisms I may possess. To discern which charism
I may actually have was the challenging part of the process.

One of my suggested charisms was writing. My first impres-
sion was that it had to be wrong because I struggled with English
in school and spelling was not my strong suit. Angela would have
definitely agreed. I remember one afternoon when I was assisting
the twins with their English homework, I made a revelation and
announced, "Listen boys, let me give you some help. Almost all

---

[10] Marianne Williamson, *A Return to Love: Reflections on the Principles of A Course
in Miracles* (NY, Harper Collins, 1992), Chapter 7, Section 3, pp.190–191.

words have a vowel in them!" Angela started giggling and replied, "What? All words have a vowel in them. No wonder why your kids are struggling." We continued to crack up over that story for years.

However, charisms are not about us but rather God working through us in order to reach someone in a positive way. There were several questions about each charism to help determine if they were a match. One question about writing was, Have you ever written something that brought tears to someone's eyes? Or has your writing moved someone emotionally? I had to think about these questions and reach out to friends and family for their answers. I have always written cards to friends and family members ever since I was a young girl. I felt drawn to writing as a therapeutic way of healing. Then those four words that my sister Debra said to me after I read Angela's eulogy came to me again, "You have a gift." Was writing my supernatural charism gift from God?

Over the next few weeks, we were asked to practice the charism to see what would happen. It was sort of like performing mini experiments to discern if indeed it was a true charism. I decided to buy blank greeting cards. I did not know to whom I was writing the cards but I felt the Holy Spirit would guide me. After Mass, I felt compelled to write to a coworker. She kept popping into my mind throughout the day. I did not know her that well, but I knew she was a single parent dealing with some struggles.

I did feel apprehensive about writing to her. I didn't know what I was going to write, so I kept procrastinating. On Sunday, I could not stop thinking of her. The Holy Spirit was nudging me to write that day and it could not wait. Reluctantly, I took out the card and just wrote from my heart. Honestly, I do not remember exactly what I wrote, except that it was words of encouragement. The miracle of a charism is that the Holy Spirit will guide you.

When I got to work on Tuesday, I felt uncomfortable giving her the card. I knew I had to give her the card. I mustered up the courage to hand her the card at the end of the day. I told her that I wrote her a note from God. I didn't know how she would respond or if she would think I was out of my mind.

Instead she replied, "Oh, thank you. Is it a sympathy card for my brother?"

I replied, "No, it is just a card for you."

She told me her brother passed away a few years ago and Sunday was the anniversary of his passing. She had been with her family at the cemetery. Chills ran up my spine because I had no knowledge of this. I left the office in total awe of God.

The next morning at work, she pulled me aside and told me that was the nicest, sweetest card she had ever received. Through her tears, she confessed that on Sunday before visiting the cemetery, she went to church alone. She was deeply troubled. During Mass, she asked God for some kind of sign to let her know that he loves her. She told me that the card was her proof.

CHAPTER 26

Each year the Centering Prayer group created its own annual Centering Prayer Retreat. For the fourth retreat, I felt guided by the Holy Spirit to write the opening prayer. This was the prayer I wrote.

An Invitation From God

To each of you here today, I just want to say how delighted I am that you have chosen to spend the day with me. My heart bursts with joy at the sight of each of you, the same joy a parent feels when a child chooses to spend time with them.

My soul was filled with ecstatic anticipation waiting for you to arrive and knowing you wanted to be with me, the same anticipation new love feels longing to embrace each other.

I just want you to know how amazing you are.

It may have been the time you hugged a crying child.

It may have been the time you donated your time and resources.

It may have been the time you comforted someone in need.

It may have been the time you prayed for others.

It may have been the time you sat diligently at one's bedside.

It may have been the time you brightened someone's day with a smile.

But did you know that each act of kindness you deepened your connection not only with them but also with me?

Your presence here today, by accepting my invitation to be with me to renew and strengthen our love, is a true gift.

With eternal love,
Your heavenly Father

When the time approached the following year for our next retreat, I knew this was the year I would share. The retreat was usually scheduled in September, but for some reason, it had to be changed to October. I felt the courage to go to the leaders to explain that I felt spiritually called to be the speaker at the next retreat and they were delighted. We set up a meeting to discuss the theme for the retreat.

During the planning meeting, we used a theme from Joyce Rupp's book, *The Cup of Our Life*.[11] The beginning of our retreat was focused on the empty cup representing coming to the retreat empty and open to receiving God. The last part of the retreat was focused on the full cup, as we leave the retreat filled with God's love.

Each person attending was asked to bring a personal cup with them. I brought the coffee cup I gave my father many years ago. It had a picture of a dog in a lounge chair watching television with the caption, "Life is so hard. It's breathe, breathe, breathe all the time." My father would always joke about that as he struggled with his breathing. Nicole also attended the retreat to support me. The cup

---

[11] Joyce Rupp, O.S.M., *The Cup of Our Life* (IN, Ave Maria Press, 1997), pp.65–67.

she brought was the cup my sister received when Nicole was born. The cup's caption was "New Mommy." That was Angela's favorite cup. I would always joke telling her that she is not a new mommy anymore, since Nicole was an adult. Both cups brought back fond memories for each of us.

The middle portion of the retreat was focused on the chipped cup. This was my portion of the retreat. The retreatants were invited to reflect on how sometimes their life can be like a chipped cup. We all have times in our lives when our cups may not be perfect. Our cups may be damaged with small chips or big dents. I shared with the group the segment of my life when my cup was severely fractured and how Centering Prayer was the glue that held my cup together.

I am bringing this portion of my life and this book to a close with this presentation which I gave at the retreat. It is a summary of everything I experienced. It was the first time I gave public witness to my story and God's action in my life.

My mother was an only child, and my father had only one brother who was a priest. However, they created a large loving family of their own. We were raised with strong family values focused on religion, hard work and education. My family also shared a unique sense of humor and lots of laughter. Religion is an important part of our lives, but I was always drawn to the more spiritual side. I always found comfort in God, nature and my extreme love for animals. I grew up strong and independent. It may have been the effects of growing up in the sixties and seventies in New York, or it may have been just who I am.

I am truly blessed with a close-knit family. We still go on family vacations together. My family is the most important thing in my life. I have two brothers and two sisters, but I was the closest to my oldest sister. We were constantly together, and growing up, I would follow her around like a puppy. Anyone who met us could easily see how close we were. My sister had three children and her daughter Nicole and I shared a very similar bond.

About ten years ago, I decided to move to Virginia with my husband and twin boys. I wanted to give my sons a better life including a new house and nicer schools. We took a chance and built a house and moved without jobs. It was a gamble for us and we had never done anything like this before. I felt pulled to do this. My husband and I had good jobs. We were surrounded by our loving family, friends and neighbors. We were not leaving New York for any negative reasons. It was hard for us and our children because we were so close to our family and friends. My children grew up with my sister's and brother's children. We established a new life here and continued to live a balanced life focused on family, work and fun.

Then my life changed with a phone call from my niece Nicole. I knew instantly something was very wrong. She told me my sister suffered a major stroke and had no control over half her body. She was on life support and later diagnosed with advanced incurable lung cancer. The tumor was central in her chest with multiple large lymph nodes compressing her circulation and breathing. That was just the beginning of the horror to come. She was on life support for over seven weeks unable to eat or speak and in and out of consciousness.

She was able to manage to write a bit and wrote a message to me. She wrote that she wanted me and my husband to raise her son and that she had a legal will stating so. At the time, her daughters were eighteen and twenty-two and her son was twelve. I knew she wanted me to be the legal guardian of her children if something would happen to her. But I also knew the law will not allow this if there is still another living parent. Of course, I promised her I would do everything in my power to raise her son and care for her two daughters.

For weeks, I was her advocate because she could not speak. I was now her watchdog trying to comfort her and care for her. I was very protective when she was able to fall asleep, I would not let anyone disturb her. She suffered and endured so much and no one should have to endure what she went through. My patience was tested as I sat there for hours waiting for any results. Once I saw the CAT scan, I knew just how severe her health was. It felt like my heart was being ripped out of me, but my heartbreak would become even worse. In the hospital, my nieces started opening up to me about their father and their homelife.

I knew that my brother-in-law had drinking and drug issues but not the severity of his addictions. I soon learned about his gambling addiction and money he owed. My sister put up a good front and hid very well the details surrounding her husband.

My sister was the total opposite of her husband. She was a powerhouse, a caring mother, hard worker and very responsible. She loved her family and friends and was full of personality and laughter. But she was naive to the world of drugs and gambling and didn't want people to know the dark secrets of their marriage. She felt she had a handle on him but that wasn't so. My sister was for me my support system, my second mother and my best friend. Listening and learning about all the despicable things that my brother-in-law put her and her children through made me emotionally ill. It was no wonder why she was lying here dying in the hospital.

The following weeks brought about a lot of drama and shocking details involving my brother-in-law. He was constantly high and rarely came to the hospital. He would spend all the money and expect my nieces to work and pay the bills. They took care of my nephew while he went out all night long.

The more I learned and witnessed, the more upset and angry I became while feeling so distraught over the declining health of my sister. I had to stay calm around my brother-in-law because I witnessed what happened when he was being confronted. He would get loud and ballistic, yelling to throw focus away from him. I didn't want him to view me as an enemy.

I stayed at my sister's house during this time to keep an eye on them. I remembered before going to the hospital one day, I was crumpled on the floor of the shower crying and cried out to God, "Why is this happening?" In my ear, I heard a crystal clear voice saying, "*Save the children.*" I knew it was God and I now understood why this was happening. I nodded my head and I accepted his call. I found the strength to stand up and get dressed and went back to the hospital.

After several weeks in New York, I decided to go back to Virginia with my nephew. My niece took a leave from her job and stood watch at my sister's bedside. I took my nephew with me which would give my niece a break and would allow my nephew to spend time with my sons. The three boys were always close and more like brothers than cousins. I knew at this point that my sister would never leave the hospital. I kept in constant contact with her doctors and nurses and updates on the hour from my family. I was looking into getting family leave and deciding when to return to New York.

I prayed the rosary every day and spoke to God constantly. I asked God to wait until I returned to New York before she died, but if he needed to take her sooner, I would understand. She was now in multiorgan failure and rapidly declining. My brother-in-law was listed as the first name on her health care proxy and I was the second contact name if he was unavailable. There were several occasions when he was not reachable and I had to make decisions on her behalf. I knew she would not want to continue like this. Her body was shutting down, dialysis was unsuccessful, and her hand was gangrenous. The doctors wanted to amputate.

Her husband kept refusing to sign the DNR (Do Not Resuscitate) form because he wanted to keep her alive for financial reasons. I pleaded with the nurse that if my brother-in-law showed up to try to persuade him to sign the DNR. On the day I decided to fly back to New York with my nephew, I received a call from the nurse. He told me that my brother-in-law finally signed the paper. I felt some relief but then felt overwhelming sadness flying back to New York with my nephew knowing that his mother who loved him so much was going to die very soon.

When I arrived at the hospital, I was shocked to see the condition my sister was in. I had the nurses remove the tape from her eyes. I sat with her crying, talking, praying and hugging her until she died.

The events and the year that followed were nothing short of a living hell for me. Our normal grieving process was stolen from us because of the chaos created by my brother-in-law. He was no longer under my sister's watch, and his behavior was even more out of control. He spent every penny on drinking and gambling binges leaving my nieces to work and to take care of everything.

I was in a panic, leaving her children alone with him knowing the dangers of his lifestyle. He did agree that my nephew could live with me but then changed his mind because he didn't want to lose the social security money that my nephew was receiving.

I am type A personality and I want everything done as quickly and efficiently as possible. I thought I was extremely patient in the hospital, but my patience was truly tested in the following year. I was imprisoned with anxiety and worry over the welfare of my sister's children while dealing with the overwhelming sadness and grief of losing my beloved sister.

I do believe God gave me sustaining power to continue. So I continued to go to work and every free minute all I could do was pray and cry. I went into my tough New York warrior mode to help the children. I had to get out of my comfort zone dealing with lawyers, private investigators, social workers, schools and Child Protective Services. My brother-in-law is smart, cunning and a master manipulator. My mind was obsessed with figuring out every angle and how to plan out each unpredictable outcome in order to get custody of my nephew.

Family and lifelong friends who lived in New York near the children offered little help. No one wanted to deal with my brother-in-law. Old wounds that I thought were healed reopened allowing even more pain. Maybe I was too much for them to handle or maybe they were in their own grief, but no one wanted to get involved. At this point, I was obsessed with doing everything humanly possible to fulfill my promise to my sister.

I felt a tremendous amount of pressure. I had the lives of my sister's children whom I love so much in my hands. The girls had to put their trust and faith in me during this time. I had to ask them to make very difficult choices, not knowing what the outcome would be. Both of my nieces have shown extreme strength and courage and did everything I asked of them out of love for their brother and mother. They were in such distress and sorrow while living with a father who could be explosive and intimidating.

Both girls had to move out of the house they grew up in and leave their brother behind. It was the only way Child Protective Services could get involved. Child Protective Services' hands were tied if there were any other adults in the house who could take care of my nephew. We had to leave my nephew alone with his father and wait to let things unfold. The girls had to escape at night while their father was out. One of my nieces went into hiding. This was the start of weeks and months to pass just waiting and waiting.

My mind was frantic twenty-four hours a day. Every minute I was awake and during all my sleepless nights, I was expecting the next upsetting phone call from my niece regarding my nephew's welfare. My nephew was being left alone for days at a time. I was obsessed with carefully documenting every event, which could be helpful in court. I became the puppet master pulling strings from Virginia to get things moving in New York while trying to plan out every move. It was exhausting and stressful. There were many days when I was on the "edge of the ledge," but I held on waiting to see what the next twenty-four hours would bring. At this point, there were ex-cons and drug dealers living in the house with my nephew. My nephew was being neglected, he was filthy, and he was missing a tremendous amount of school.

I was now in a fragile state of mind with all the stress and worry. I felt broken. There were two times when I was on the brink of a nervous breakdown. I heard from my lawyer and Child Protective Services that I was going to get custody, but then the decision was reversed. My nephew would tell the truth when Child Protective Services came to visit, but unfortunately once coached by his father, he would lie to protect him. So I had to continue to wait several more months for the court custody date.

My brother-in-law was a tornado and I was in the center of it. I then realized that my brother-in-law was weak and a coward. He allowed evil to take hold of him and evil was enjoying my suffering. I know evil is strong but I also know God is more powerful, so I had to find ways to pull myself away from this storm before it was too late. I just wanted peace in my mind. It took all my strength just to go to work. I would urgently run to get into my car and within seconds burst into tears. My car was my safe haven where I could cry and scream driving home every day from work. I would cry out over and over to God, "Please help me!" I realized one day in my car while driving that no one could comfort me but only God, for he is the only one who truly knew my pain. My pain was unique to me and I had to trust God as my ultimate healer.

I found a Christian radio station and felt comfort listening to the music. I felt God sent me a direct message through a song. The song was "Before the Morning" by Josh Wilson. The lyrics brought me hope especially the words,

> So hold on,
> You gotta wait for the light,
> Press on and just fight the good fight
> 'Cause the pain that you've been feeling,
> it's the dark before the morning.[12]

I felt the most at peace in my car listening to the music. The words in the songs were soothing to me. I felt close to God in my car and God had become my best friend.

I was realizing I could not prevent things from happening but only how I responded to them. I knew I felt connected to God at church, so I wanted to deepen that connection. I started going to counseling, classes, retreats and other resources offered at the church. I went to a Lenten Retreat that year. During the retreat, we were asked to read a scripture and then sit in silence. We were told to make a sacred quiet place in our home and just sit with God. So I did that every night. I sat with God in silence. It was during this time that I truly felt God's love and

---

[12] Josh Wilson, *Life is not a Snapshot Label (Sparrow Records, 9/4/2009)*.

God's presence physically in me. I began feeling more connected to God. It was truly amazing to feel God's love and peace. Words cannot express the feeling that overtook me. I was feeling reborn knowing that my old life had died and my life was being transformed.

I was thirsty to learn more. I started reading books, going to more classes, and began writing. I was getting out of my comfort zone, but with each experience, I was feeling more peace. I went to the Centering Prayer workshop and joined our first Centering Prayer group meeting. Even at this point, I didn't think a group would help, but God nudged me to go to the Centering Prayer group. Now I was listening and feeling his direction for me to move. I realized that during the Lenten Retreat, I was centering before I even knew what Centering Prayer was. I began feeling the healing power of God.

During the Sunday Mass before the upcoming court date, the words, "Thy Will" really touched me. After Mass, I spoke to my niece and I could hear the distress in her voice as she too was on the verge of a nervous breakdown. I told her, "Nicole, stop whatever you are doing right now and just find the closest church to you." She did just that and we both realized at this point that we did all that we could humanly have done and now it was God's will, not ours, to determine the outcome for my nephew.

We went to court, and by the grace of God, I got joint custody of my nephew having him reside with me. Getting custody of my nephew was bittersweet because I had to take him from the only home he knew. Centering Prayer helped me with the many struggles that surfaced with raising my nephew. He showed signs of neglect, was withdrawn and was in an emotional state of an eight-year-old. We had to address these physical and emotional issues.

My husband was truly amazing during all of this, and he did every chore or errand I asked of him without a single complaint. He loved my sister and her children very much. My sons were an essential part of my nephew's healing because they gave him security, brotherhood and friendship. My nieces moved to Virginia and we all worked together as a new nucleus to rebuild our family.

I thought God moved me to Virginia because of my children. Then I thought God moved us to Virginia for the safety of my sister's children, and now I realized God moved me to Virginia to help me because God loves me as well.

I am proud to say my nephew is now a junior in college. All the children are doing well and are well adjusted. I feel so blessed that God allowed me the privilege to continue to raise my sister's children with my husband. When people ask me if I have children, I joke and say, "Yes, I have five children, all different ages, but only one pregnancy."

I tell people Centering Prayer saved me and it really did. Through Centering Prayer, God brought me calmness, peace, healing, restoration and love. I'm so grateful and blessed for the kindness, encouragement and friendship found in our Centering Prayer group. I would now like to end my presentation by sharing with you a piece that I was guided by God to write.

Safely to Shore

It was like someone flipped a switch and all my light was stripped away, leaving me in total darkness. Panic, shock, and confusion gripped my body, mind and soul. I was alone stranded in the midst of darkness struggling to keep my head above the cold dark water that surrounded me. How could my life change so drastically in a second?

So I drifted and drifted, day turning into night and night turning into day.

Exhaustion quickly took hold of me, but then in the distance, like a vision, I saw a boat approaching. Hope and relief washed over me. I was going to be saved. I couldn't believe my eyes on the boat were family and friends. I heard them calling my name. I saw them waving at me. I started waving and shouting back until a wave took me under. As I surfaced, I felt a new level of hopelessness, pain and rage. The boat that I thought was help started moving farther and farther away from me.

So I just drifted and drifted.

I was truly alone and numb. Waves of despair crashed over me with no glimmer of hope. I cried out begging God over and over again, "Please help me." So I prayed and leaned on God for he was the only one who truly knew my pain. I came to accept my reality but continued to struggle. I knew now everything was indeed in God's hands.

So I just drifted and drifted.

I had to learn to try to calm my mind and trust in God to help me stay afloat. My mind would be riddled with fear and panic with the reality of the evil forces and dangers that lurked below me, knowing how easily I could be pulled under, kicking and fighting with all my might, gulping water and gasping for air knowing that the next time may be my final time.

So I just drifted and drifted.

I was getting weaker and weaker as life was depleted from me. I felt my body slip under the water. Something gently nudged me, and I managed to throw my arm around it. Total exhaustion consumed me physically, emotionally and mentally but now I felt something had changed. I felt a slight curl on my lip trying to smile, for I realized I was no longer floating but beneath me was solid ground.

Centering Prayer was my life preserver which gently pulled the rope that brought me safely to shore.

I knew in my heart that one day, I would be standing here sharing as part of my healing process. I am a firm believer in signs, and when I heard the retreat date was changed to October 20, that was the catalyst I needed. Today is October 20 (10/20). It is a very important date and number to me. Today is my sister Angela's birthday and it is also the exact time my sister left my loving arms and was delivered into the loving arms of our Lord.

Silence hung in the air as I concluded my sharing at the retreat. I looked up from the podium immediately and made eye contact with Nicole. As I scanned the room looking at the faces of those present, I could see how touched and moved they were. Listening to their feedback, I was inspired to write this book. This season of my life was not easy. It was through God's love and friendship that I was able to survive this traumatic time in my life.

Of course, it was not a quick fix. It took determination and devotion on my behalf and listening to God's direction. With each class I attended, book I read, or prayer I prayed, I was blessed with enrichment from each experience. God is there for all of us every moment of every day. God took my chipped cup when it was empty, filled it and restored me. God will fill your cup when empty and restore you when your cup is chipped.

EPILOGUE

The Forecast

I step outside; my eyes squint from the brightness of the sun.
I smile at the sight of the most beautiful crystal clear blue sky.
I take a slow deep inhale and feel God's joy enter my soul.
I step outside and cringe at the looming dark
dismal sky with its gray threatening clouds.
I then think of God's protective ways and it eases my anxious mind.
I step outside into the cool night air and I'm
mesmerized by the dark blanket that covers the
sky, glimmering with all its tiny little lights.
I sense God's calmness and a wave of serenity
filters into every pore of my body.
I step outside and shiver from the cold harsh temperature.
I'm taken aback from the force of a brutal
slap of wind across my face.
I then feel the healing touch of God's embrace
that brings warmth to my heart.
No matter what type of weather I may endure,
God is with me through every season of my life.

Kate Lynn Winters

ACKNOWLEDGEMENT

O ne of my son's favorite inspirational quotes by Lorri Faye is, "Even a single thread of hope is still a very powerful thing." When I found my life unraveling, I held tightly to God's thread and was so grateful for his presence.

I want to thank God for his guidance and how he blessed me with the love and endearing friendship from my Centering Prayer mentors.

I also want to sincerely thank my husband, sons, my family and especially Nicole and Amanda, my nieces for their love, support and encouragement that they had shown me throughout my life and during the process of writing, *The Chipped Cup.*

I am forever grateful for my nephew Tommy's perseverance during this dark journey we traveled together as he continues to bring light into my life. I am also blessed to witness my sister's children as they live their lives with kindness and compassion, keeping my sister Angela's legacy alive.

THOUGHTS TO PONDER

These questions have been created for your quiet prayer reflection, journaling, or use in a small group setting.

1. Were you inspired by or felt connected to any part of Kate's journey?
2. Do you have a particular prayer, psalm, or inspirational quote that resonates with you?
3. Have you ever thought of seeking spiritual direction, and did Kate's choice influence you to consider that more seriously?
4. Do you have a prayer group in your life? If yes, how does it strengthen your faith journey? If no, would you consider joining one since you have read Kate's book?
5. We all have times in our life when we feel our life is like a chipped cup. Recall a time in your life when you felt this way, and whom did you ask for help?
6. Kate believes signs can be a message from God and has become attuned to them in her life. Have you ever had a similar experience?
7. Nicole and Amanda, Kate's nieces, had the courage to trust their aunt's guidance. Is there someone in your life you trust to that extent?

8. During a devastating time in her life, Kate received a calling from God: "Save the children." Have you ever received a calling, and how did you respond?

9. Kate's patience was tested as she exhausted all her efforts to "Save the children." She spiritually understood the situation was out of her hands and truly in the hands of God. Have you experienced a similar moment in your life?

10. Mental anguish pushed Kate to a tipping point on the verge of a nervous breakdown. Centering Prayer grounded her in prayer and her relationship with God. Does your prayer life help you cope in times of struggle and despair?

11. Kate mentions how even in the darkest moments, beautiful moments can arise. Describe an experience when you felt blessed during a challenge in your life?

12. Forgiveness was sometimes a struggle for Kate, but she learned that not forgiving would be detrimental to her healing process. Is there someone in your life you need to forgive?

13. Kate learned that she had to "let go" of her old life for her "new life" to emerge. Are you holding on to something in your life that needs to be surrendered?

14. The last line of Kate's reflection, "The Wise Men," Kate writes, "But if you think about it, if you really look deep into someone's eyes, you too will see God, for God is in all of us." In whose eyes do you see God? When have you witnessed God's love through the actions of others?

15. The book concludes with Kate's poem, "The Forecast," where she describes God's presence in the good times as well as the struggles in her life. During those times in your life, when do you feel God's presence the strongest?

BIBLIOGRAPHY

Clifton, Ph.D., Donald O. Liesveld, M. Div., M.A., Winseman, D. Min., Albert L. *Living Your Strengths*. NY: Gallup Press, 2006.

Contemplative Outreach Ltd. *The Method of Centering Prayer The Prayer of Consent*. NJ: Contemplative Outreach Ltd. 2006.

Contemplative Outreach Ltd. *Contemplative Outreach News*. NJ: Contemplative Outreach Ltd. 2013.

Keating. O.C.S.O., *Thomas, Open Mind, Open Heart*. NY: Amity House, 2006.

Meninger, O.C.S.O., William A. *The Process of Forgiveness*. NY: Bloomsbury, 1996.

Merrill, Nan C., *Psalms for Praying*. NY: Continuum, 1996.

Rupp, O.S.M., Joyce, *The Cup of Our Life*. IN: Ave Maria Press, 1997.

ABOUT THE AUTHOR

Kate Lynn Winters was born and raised in New York with her large traditional Catholic family. She has a long-standing career in the medical field. Later in life, she moved to Virginia with her husband and twin sons. After the tragic death of her beloved sister, she was able to gain custody of her nephew. Her nieces moved as well to join their brother. Kate now considers herself a mother of five.

She enjoys spending time with all her family members, especially with her creative themed parties. Besides her love for her family, she has always had a strong affection for animals and nature. She volunteers with special needs children as a religious education catechist. The privilege of working with these children led her to start and coordinate a special needs social ministry at her church.

After Kate spoke at a religious retreat for her prayer group, she was inspired to write, *The Chipped Cup*. In her book, she shares her journey through a dark, painful time in her life with the intention to shine hope and light to others.

CPSIA information can be obtained
at www.ICGtesting.com
Printed in the USA
JSHW021501190822
29483JS00001B/65